CELEBRATING SPECIAL DAYS
IN THE CHURCH SCHOOL YEAR

LITURGIES AND PARTICIPATION ACTIVITIES FOR CHURCH SCHOOL CHILDREN

BY JUDY GATTIS SMITH

To the children and workers of Windsor Hills United Methodist Church, Roanoke, Virginia — a special group who helped make many of these "special days" happen.

— Judy Gattis Smith

MERIWETHER PUBLISHING LTD.
COLORADO SPRINGS, COLORADO

Meriwether Publishing, Ltd., Publisher
885 Elkton Drive
Colorado Springs, CO 80907

edited by Catherine A. Zeiss
cover design by Michelle Zapel

ISBN: 0-916260-14-3
© Copyright MCMLXXXI Meriwether Publishing Ltd.
Printed in the United States of America
Second Edition
Library of Congress #81-83441

FORWARD

Our Church Year is garlanded with "Special Days." Seasons and festivals, sacraments and other rites of the church add depth and meaning to our Christian experience. No one would deny the impact of Christmas or Easter in the life of a church or church school. But there are many other Special Days — occasions for richly varied Bible-centered celebrations.

The purpose of this book is to present some of these Special Days in ways that children will find meaningful. The programs involve active participation by the children so that they are not only being taught the faith but become a part of the faith story.

Occasions in the life of a child such as the beginning of school, the presentation of Bibles to third graders and the experience of moving to a new community are seen as part of our Christian pilgrimage.

Sometimes these Special Days are celebrated with the entire church family in the sanctuary, as children join adults in congregational worship. Sometimes these Special Day celebrations are more informal and may include eating together. A fellowship hall is usually the setting at these times. Again, some Special Days must be experienced out-of-doors or in the more intimate setting of a small classroom.

Wherever they are set, the purpose is to entwine the everyday life experiences of the Church School children with the on-going story of our Faith. Using our rich Bible heritage, our common traditions and our passed-down hopes, struggles and dreams, children will learn, through liturgies and participation activities, who they are and the meaning of their lives. The story of their ancestors in the faith will become their story, with meaning and impact.

Judy Gattis Smith

Listen my people to my teaching! Pay attention to what I say.
I am going to use wise sayings and explain mysteries from the past;
things we have heard and known; things that our fathers told us.
We will not keep them from our children. We will tell the next
generation about the Lord's power and his great deeds and the
wonderful things he has done.

Psalms 78: 1-4

TABLE OF CONTENTS

NOTES

Copyright Information

Most of the Biblical passages in this book are quoted from the **Good News Bible.** If there is no other indication, they are from this source. The **Good News Bible** — Old Testament: copyright ©American Bible Society, 1976; New Testament: copyright ©American Bible Society, 1966, 1971, 1976.

The Methodist Hymnal, the Methodist Publishing Co., 1966, is used as a source for hymns throughout this book. Most of these hymns can be readily found in hymnals of other denominations as well.

Music Source Suggestions

All hymns and songs indicated in this book are suggestions only. They are chosen to fit the mood of the material being presented. A source is given for all suggested hymns and songs. Other hymns or songs may be substituted as desired.

How to Use this Book

When you plan to use one of the activities in this book, look over all the material well ahead of the time of performance. Read through the *entire* liturgy or program to find out what is involved. Take note of the music, props, costumes, number of participants and/or materials required.

Most of these activities and liturgies require some preparation in the form of planning, material gathering and rehearsal. Be sure you have the music indicated or appropriate substitutions well in advance.

Avoid unnecessary surprises at the last minute. Studying the complete section of the activity you have chosen is important to knowing exactly what you will need.

FALL
SEPTEMBER/OCTOBER/NOVEMBER

SPECIAL DAYS IN FALL

There is a crispness in the air. There is a surge of energy. There is a sense of starting something new and exciting. It is Fall in the Church School. Regular Church School classes are starting, but the celebration of some Special Days can highlight this season of eager beginnings.

Capitalize on this eagerness with a special service honoring 3rd graders receiving their Bibles. Recognize where childrens' thoughts are, with a special children's liturgy for the beginning of school. Honor the church school teachers who are dedicating themselves to a year of service with a special dinner.

Then as Halloween rolls around, join with the whole church in a dinner dedicated to "Celebrating Our Children." Enter the sanctuary at Thanksgiving with a children's liturgy of praise. And observe National Bible Week by reading the Bible without ceasing in a special all-day service.

Promotion Sunday — Presentation of Bibles to 3rd Graders

INTRODUCTION

The presentation of Bibles to children entering the third grade is a common practice in many of our churches. But too often this special occasion has become a perfunctory event. We are showing a lack of concern if we make the presentation of Bibles just a passing out of books and a "performance" by the children. This is a significant experience, a jubilee and a tremendous occasion for celebration! Here are children just feeling comfortable with reading, just knowing the excitement of unlocking the secrets of books, just taking that first step of being "grown up" in the church. Here are children filled with vitality and imagination, anxious to develop learning skills, susceptible to wonder and mystery. How can we gather up all of this in a service of meaning and dignity? Following is a service of celebration for the presentation of Bibles.

PARTICIPANTS

Children
Church School Superintendent or other Adult
Minister
Congregation

MATERIALS

small chest or decorative box
pulpit-size Bible
wrappings: brown paper, gold foil, colored comic strip paper, white tissue
bookmarks
cake for reception (Bible-shape, optional)

SOURCES FOR MUSIC SUGGESTIONS

"The Bible Is a Treasure Book" — **Rejoice and Sing Praise,** compiled by Evelyn Andre and Jeneil Menefee, Abingdon Press, 1977.
"Doxology" also called "Praise God From Whom All Blessings Flow" — found in most hymnals

LITURGY

Bible Unwrapping

INSTRUCTIONS — The children to receive Bibles have gathered in the narthex or back of the church. The organ begins a processional hymn, such as "The Bible Is a Treasure Book." (FROM **REJOICE AND SING PRAISE**, ABINGDON PRESS, 1977)

Two older children enter first, carrying a chest, preferably a small one with handles on each side, containing a specially wrapped, pulpit-size Bible. All children to receive Bibles process behind the chest containing the Bible. The older children present the chest to the minister at the front of the church, who places it on the altar table. The children stand in front of the altar.

MINISTER: Today is a very special day in the life of this congregation. We have come together to worship God and to present Bibles to our third grade students. Boys and girls, you have reached a special time in your church life. You have heard Bible stories read to you, you have looked at pictures in Bible story books, you have memorized Bible verses. But now the time has come for you to have your very own Bible, to read these stories and discover the Christian faith for yourself and to experience the truths of these stories. We, the congregation, rejoice with you in this special time of church growth and we now pass on to you this valuable treasure — the book of our Faith.

(MINISTER REMOVES BIBLE FROM CHEST. IT IS WRAPPED IN BROWN WRAPPING PAPER. MINISTER HANDS BIBLE TO SUPERINTENDENT OR OTHER ADULT)

ADULT: Our treasure is wrapped in brown wrapping paper to remind you that this is a very old book. This is a book of 30 centuries. Can you imagine how long 30 centuries is? Some parts of this book were composed more than a thousand years before Christ. Some of the stories are so old they were told even before people knew how to write.

(ADULT HANDS BIBLE TO MINISTER WHO FACES ALTAR AND HOLDS THE BOOK HIGH)

MINISTER: Praise God for this ancient treasure.

CONGREGATION: We do praise and thank God for our Bible.

(MINISTER HANDS BOOK BACK TO ADULT, WHO WITH THE HELP OF ONE OR MORE THIRD GRADE CHILD, CAREFULLY REMOVES THE LAYER OF BROWN WRAPPING PAPER. UNDERNEATH IS A LAYER OF GOLD FOIL. THE BIBLE IS NOW WRAPPED IN GOLD FOIL)

ADULT: We think of gold as the most valuable thing there is, but this treasure is more valuable than gold because it is a source of truth and guidance for our lives and even gold cannot buy these things. Men have died to save this book. They have been imprisoned because they read it. In some churches, to show how much this book is valued, people decorate it with jewels.

(ADULT HANDS BIBLE TO MINISTER WHO AGAIN FACES ALTAR, RAISES BOOK AND SAYS)

MINISTER: Praise God for this valuable treasure.

CONGREGATION: We do praise and thank God for our Bible.

(MINISTER HANDS BOOK TO ADULT. ADULT AND ANOTHER THIRD GRADE CHILD CAREFULLY REMOVE THE LAYER OF GOLD WRAPPING TO FIND THE BIBLE WRAPPED IN COLORED, COMIC STRIP PAPER)

ADULT: This is a book of stories. Some of the best stories in the world are found in this book: Joseph in the pit, Daniel in the lions' den, Moses receiving the Ten Commandments on the high mountain, Paul shipwrecked.

And we will wonder — What did the story mean to the very first people who ever heard it? Why did people think this story was so important that it must be written down? What do the stories mean for your life?

(ADULT HANDS BOOK TO MINISTER WHO FACES ALTAR AND RAISES BOOK)

MINISTER: Praise God for the stories of our faith.

CONGREGATION: We do praise and thank God for our Bible.

(MINISTER HANDS BIBLE TO ADULT. WITH HELP OF STILL ANOTHER THIRD GRADER, THEY UNWRAP THE LAYER OF COMIC STRIP PAPER AND FIND THE BIBLE WRAPPED IN A LAYER OF WHITE TISSUE PAPER)

ADULT: The Bible is an inspired book. It came from a people who had a special understanding of God. Therefore it is not like any other book you will ever own. When you read it you will understand what God is like and what he wants you to do. In the Bible we have a message from God and about God.

(ADULT HANDS BIBLE TO MINISTER WHO FACES ALTAR, ELEVATING THE BIBLE)

MINISTER: Praise God for this inspired book.

CONGREGATION: We do praise and thank God for our Bible.

(BIBLE IS PLACED ON ALTAR TABLE)

Presentation of Bibles

ADULT: And now, we pass our treasure on to you. Will you step forward as your name is read to receive your very own Bible, a gift from this church family to you.

(MINISTER OR ADULT READS NAMES OF CHILDREN WHO STEP FORWARD AND RECEIVE THEIR BIBLES. AT THE END OF THIS, THE CONGREGATION MAY RISE AND SING)

ALL SING: "Doxology" also called "Praise God from Whom All Blessings Flow" (FOUND IN MOST HYMNALS)

MINISTER: Each of you third graders will find a marker in your Bible. Will you now open your Bible to the page that is marked? On this page you will find certain words colored with a yellow marking pencil. Will you read these words with me now as the Scripture Lesson for the day.
(NOTE: IF YOU DON'T WISH TO MARK IN THE BIBLES, YOU CAN NOTE THE PASSAGE YOU WISH TO HAVE READ BY WRITING THE BOOK AND VERSE NUMBER ON THE BOOK-MARK USED)

THIRD GRADERS: (READ TOGETHER) Jesus increased in wisdom and in stature, and in favor with God and man. (Luke 2:52 Revised Standard Version)

MINISTER: These holy words are our wish for you. May you also grow in wisdom and stature and favor with God and man.

(CHILDREN MAY NOW JOIN THEIR PARENTS IN THE CONGREGATION)

(THE REMAINDER OF THE CHURCH SERVICE SHOULD FOLLOW A THEME OF CHRISTIAN GROWTH OR THE BIBLE)

Reception

You might wish to continue your celebration by having a reception following the service in honor of the third graders. They could be congratulated by the congregation in a receiving line.

Each child might share a Bible verse that he or she has chosen to be his or her own special verse for the year. The children should pick out these verses before the day of the Bible presentation.

Refreshments might also be served at this informal reception. A special cake baked in the shape of a Bible would be unique and appropriate.

Liturgy for the Beginning of School

INTRODUCTION

Certainly one of the most important days of the year in the life of a child is the beginning of school. Why not recognize this fact and celebrate this occasion within the church family? Our Judeo/Christian heritage has always placed significance on acquiring knowledge. With thankfulness we celebrate minds that can learn, knowledge that can enrich life and the opportunities that are ours to "grow in wisdom and stature and favor with God and man." Following is a children's liturgy for a worship service in your sanctuary. A children's liturgy is an entire service of worship geared to children and involving children.

PARTICIPANTS

Minister, Children with textbooks

Child in back of church (also carries in Bible)

Child reader

Storyteller

Child leader (1 or more)

Congregation

People chosen from congregation

Children as money bags

MATERIALS

textbooks

green garbage bags

garbage bags stuffed with newspapers

SOURCES FOR MUSIC SUGGESTIONS

"Guide Me, O Thou Great Jehovah" — the Methodist Hymnal, No. 271.

"B-I-B-L-E" — **Action Songs for Boys and Girls,** Zondervan Publishing House, Singspiration Series.

"Tell Me the Stories of Jesus" — the Methodist Hymnal, No. 88.

"Talent Song" — from **Sing and Be Happy Songs for Children,** compiled by Alfred Smith, Rodeheaver Co., Winona Lake, IN, 46591, 1971.

"This Little Light of Mine" — **Good Times Songbook,** Abingdon Press, 1974.

ORDER OF SERVICE

Introit (Psalm 15)

Procession of children with textbooks

Blessing of textbooks with responses

Procession of Bible

Scripture (Psalm 119:9-12)

Song: "B-I-B-L-E"

Storyteller: Solomon's Dream

Responsive Sentences

Song: "Tell Me the Stories of Jesus"

Participation Parable: Story of the Talents

Children's Choir Anthem: "Talent Song"

Prayer and Offering

Recessional: "This Little Light of Mine"

LITURGY

CHILD: (FROM BACK OF CHURCH) Lord, who may enter your temple? (Psalms 15:1)

MINISTER: A person who obeys God in everything and always does what is right, whose words are true and sincere, who does not slander others. He does no wrong to his friends and does not spread rumors about his neighbors. He despises those whom God rejects, but honors those who obey the Lord. He always does what he promises, no matter how much it may cost. (Psalms 15:2-4) Those who seek to live this way are welcome to the House of the Lord.

PROCESSION: (CHILDREN ENTER, CARRYING TEXTBOOKS, AND PROCESS TO FRONT OF THE CHURCH WHILE CONGREGATION SINGS)

HYMN: "Guide Me, O Thou Great Jehovah" (THE METHODIST HYMNAL, NO. 271)

(CHILDREN HAND TEXTBOOKS TO MINISTER WHO PLACES THEM ON ALTAR. THE CHILDREN ARE SEATED IN THE CONGREGATION)

MINISTER: We come before God today at a special time of the year — the beginning of school. Each child has brought a textbook that he or she will be using this year — science, math, English. It is good that, just as the Scripture tells us about Jesus, we seek to grow in wisdom. Will you join now in the blessing of these books?

Here, Father, are some of the books we will be studying this year.

CONGREGATION: Bless we pray the learning and the learners.

MINISTER: You have given us minds that question.

CONGREGATION: Bless we pray the learning and the learners.

MINISTER: Teach us to apply our hearts to wisdom.

CONGREGATION: Bless we pray the learning and the learners.

MINISTER: While we value and thank God for all these books, in our church we have a special book. Will you stand in reverence now as we bring in our Bible?

(CHILD PROCESSES IN WITH A BIBLE AND HANDS IT TO THE MINISTER. THE MINISTER RAISES IT TO THE ALTAR, ELEVATING IT IN BLESSING)

MINISTER: (contd) This is our sacred record which tells us the stories of our faith and particularly about Jesus and how he lived. We believe this book is a revelation of the Holy. (LOWERS BIBLE AND ADDRESSES CONGREGATION) Let us listen to the teaching of our sacred record.

CHILD READER: How can a young man keep his life pure? By obeying your commands. With all my heart I try to serve you. Keep me from disobeying your commandments. I keep your law in my heart so that I will not sin against you. I praise you, O Lord. Teach me your ways. (Psalms 119: 9-12)

CHILDREN'S SONG: "B-I-B-L-E" (ACTION SONGS FOR BOYS AND GIRLS, ZONDERVAN PUBLISHING HOUSE, SINGSPIRATION SERIES, OR ANOTHER ANTHEM SELECTION)

MINISTER: Father, we praise you and thank you and now, at this time of the year we also seek your guidance. We look to your Book for wisdom.

Story of Solomon

STORYTELLER: God kindly included in the Bible stories about boys. One young man in the Bible was Solomon, son of the great King David. When David died, Solomon was declared the new king. When this decision was made, Solomon had a feeling of panic. "How can I rule this mighty kingdom? I am just a child. How can I possibly rule wisely?" Though his heart was thumping, he did not tell his fears to the princes and the ambassadors and the high priests and the leaders.

There was no temple or church where he could go and pray to God, so Solomon chose a near-by mountain where a great altar stood, and there he took 1,000 offerings to burn before God. All day long he watched the burning sacrifices and as the smoke from the altar rose to the sky, Solomon prayed and prayed to God for help.

The sun set, twilight came. The great leaping flames died down to smoldering embers and still Solomon prayed. Darkness came and Solomon's eyes began to grow heavy. He sank down to sleep right where he had been praying and while he slept he had a wonderful dream. He saw God Himself standing beside him and he heard God's voice saying, "Ask whatever you wish and I will give it to you."

Can you imagine anything more wonderful — anything he wished! Well, did he want to be handsome — the ideal of physical beauty? Did he want to live to an old-old-age? Did he want to have great power over all the other kings of the world? Did he want to be fabulously wealthy? All these ideas flashed before his mind. All of these things could have been his — all he had to do was ask!

But Solomon kept remembering the great work that was his to do. He remembered how childlike he felt — how unequal to his great job. So he answered, "O Lord my God, you have made me to be King instead of my father David and I am only a child. I do not know how to rule these people.

STORYTELLER: (contd) They are the people whom you have chosen to call your own and now I ask you to give me an understanding heart so that I may know how to rule them well and that I may know right from wrong."

God was very pleased with this answer and God said, "Because you have asked for wisdom instead of asking for selfish things I am going to give you much wisdom until you will be known in every nation round about because of your great understanding and I will also give you what you have not asked for: great riches and honor I give you, so that no king in any other land while you live shall be as wise and rich and honorable as you."

And then Solomon awoke. He was still by the altar. He knew he had been dreaming, but his fears were gone now. He was sure God himself had spoken to him. He went back to Jerusalem and began to rule. And great wisdom and understanding marked everything he did and it happened just as God said in the dream. No other king was as wise or rich or honored as King Solomon who chose wisdom above all else.

(ONE OR MORE CHILDREN MAY TAKE CHILD LEADER PART)

LEADER: We need God's help as we, like Solomon, seek wisdom. Sometimes school is hard to take. I don't like sitting still that long and sometimes I feel some of the things I have to learn are dumb.

CONGREGATION: Lord have mercy and guide me.

LEADER: Some of the things we have to learn are hard and uninteresting and I forget things I am supposed to remember.

CONGREGATION: Lord have mercy and guide me.

LEADER: For giving up when I don't understand.

CONGREGATION: Lord have mercy.

LEADER: For not looking for help from my teachers or fellow classmates.

CONGREGATION: Lord have mercy.

LEADER: For forgetting to call upon God when times get tough.

CONGREGATION: Lord have mercy.

ALL: Father, it is great that we have so much to learn, but it doesn't come easy for all of us. Help us when we have difficulties not to give up and like Solomon seek above all else, wisdom and an understanding heart. Amen.

SONG: "Tell Me the Stories of Jesus" (THE METHODIST HYMNAL, NO. 88)

MINISTER: Jesus also told a story that can help us at the beginning of school. To tell this story I will need the help of some of you in the congregation.

Participation Parable — The Talents
MINISTER: Once upon a time there was a very rich man.

(MINISTER CALLS THE NAME OF SOME MAN IN THE CONGREGATION) Mr. (NAME), will you come forward and be that man? Thank you.

(MAN COMES TO FRONT OF CHURCH)

MINISTER: (contd) This man lived in the city in a fine house with many servants. He was a merchant by trade and he had gathered his great wealth by buying and selling rich and precious things from other lands. Often he had to travel abroad on his business. And travel in those days was difficult and very time consuming and dangerous. So before he left he had to make careful plans about leaving his money. What would be a wise and shrewd thing to do?

He put his money in eight moneybags. I need eight children or adults to come up and be moneybags.

(WHEN CHILDREN COME FORWARD, PLACE OVER THEM GREEN GARBAGE BAGS WITH HOLES CUT OUT FOR THEIR HEADS TO FIT THROUGH)

Here are our moneybags. Hold your elbows out so that you will be fat moneybags. Mr. (NAME), are you pleased with your money?

Next the rich man called his three most trusted servants. Will Servant 1 come forward from the congregation?

(RICH MAN MAY CALL SOMEONE BY NAME FROM THE CONGREGATION)

The man said to the servant, "There is one talent of silver in each of these bags. I am giving you five bags. Use your five talents and make as much money for me as you can."

(SERVANT TAKES FIVE MONEYBAG-CHILDREN WITH HIM AND GOES DOWN AISLE AND OUTSIDE SANCTUARY TO NARTHEX OF CHURCH)

Now we still have our rich man and three moneybags left.

(CALL SERVANT 2 FROM CONGREGATION)

To the second servant he gave two moneybags and said, "Make as much money as you can from these two talents."

(SERVANT 2 AND TWO MONEYBAG-CHILDREN GO DOWN AISLE, OUT SANCTUARY AND INTO NARTHEX OF CHURCH)

Then he called his 3rd servant.

(CALL SERVANT 3 FROM CONGREGATION)

"Here is one talent. Do the best you can with it."

(SERVANT TAKES REMAINING MONEY-BAG CHILD INTO NARTHEX)

Then the man set off on his long travels.

(RICH MAN SITS IN CHAIR AT SIDE OF ALTAR)

He had carefully instructed his three servants. They knew he would be gone a long time and that he would want a full account when he returned. The servant who had received five talents went at once and invested his money and earned another five talents. In the same way the servant who had received two talents earned another two talents. But the servant who had received one talent went off, dug a hole in the ground and hid his master's money.

MINISTER: (contd) After a long time the master of those servants came back to settle accounts with them.

(RICH MAN STANDS AND COMES BACK TO CENTER)

He calls his first servant.

(FROM BACK OF CHURCH COMES FIRST SERVANT WITH HIS FIVE MONEY-BAG CHILDREN. EACH MONEYBAG-CHILD IS CARRYING A GREEN GARBAGE BAG STUFFED WITH NEWSPAPERS)

Servant 1 returned, staggering under his heavy load of moneybags, for he had doubled his money. "Well done," said the Master. "You are a good and faithful servant. You have been faithful in managing small amounts. I will put you in charge of large amounts. Come on in and share my happiness." Then he sent for his second servant.

(SERVANT 2 COMES FROM BACK OF CHURCH WITH TWO MONEY-BAG CHILDREN. EACH MONEYBAG-CHILD CARRIES A GREEN GARBAGE BAG STUFFED WITH NEWSPAPERS)

The second servant had also doubled his money. "Well done, you good and faithful servant," said the master. "You have been faithful in managing small amounts. I will put you in charge of large amounts. Come on in and share my happiness." Next the master sent for the third servant.

(SERVANT 3 ENTERS FROM BACK OF CHURCH WITH HIS ONE, ORIGINAL MONEY-BAG CHILD, EMPTY-HANDED)

The servant said, "Sir, I know you are a hard man. You reap harvests that you did not plant and you gather crops where you did not scatter seeds. I was afraid, so I went off and hid your money in the ground. Look, here is what belongs to you."

The master was angry. "You should have deposited my money in the bank and I would have received it all back at least with interest." And he took the one moneybag and gave it to his first servant.

(ACTORS RETURN TO THEIR SEATS. CHILDREN REMOVE BAGS FROM THEIR BODIES AND SOMEONE TAKES THE EXTRA BAGS AWAY)

It is from this story that we get our word "talent." A talent is any gift we may have. There are many kinds of talents. Some are gifted with their hands, others with their brains. Every one of us has some gift from God. It is a talent that he has entrusted to us. God wants us to use our talents and to do all that we can with them. Then we find that they grow. We must not hide our talents and refuse to use them.

CHILDREN'S CHOIR: "Talent Song" (FROM **SING AND BE HAPPY SONGS FOR CHILDREN,** RODEHEAVER CO., 1971)

MINISTER: Let us pray. Heavenly Father, we are glad you know all about us because then you know what we can do best. Guide us to use our talents — digging them up, unwrapping them and multiplying them. Amen.

OFFERING OF GIFTS AND TALENTS

MINISTER: Will all the children join hands?

(TEACHER OR STUDENT LEADER TAKES HAND OF CHILD IN FIRST PEW AND LEADS CHILDREN INVOLVED IN THE PROCESSION OUT OF THE CHURCH IN A CHAIN AS THE CONGREGATION AND CHILDREN JOIN IN SINGING SUGGESTED HYMN)

HYMN: "This Little Light of Mine" (**GOOD TIMES SONGBOOK,** ABINGDON PRESS, 1974)

Teacher Appreciation Dinner

INTRODUCTION

Expressing appreciation to Church School teachers who week after week give of their time and talent is important. One way to do this is to have a special dinner in their honor. Following is the suggestion for such a program.

PARTICIPANTS

Teachers

Students

Chairperson

Leader (1 or more)

Readers 1, 2, 3, 4, 5, 6

11 Card Readers

Minister

MATERIALS

11 story cards

3 — 4 stories planned by teachers

SOURCES FOR MUSIC SUGGESTIONS

"I Love to Tell the Story" — the Methodist Hymnal, No. 149.

"Blessed Assurance" — the Methodist Hymnal, No. 224.

"Tell Me the Stories of Jesus" — the Methodist Hymnal, No. 88.

"Pass It On" — from **Tell It Like It Is**, words and music by Kurt Kaiser, Lexicon Music, Inc.

DINNER PROGRAM

WELCOME: (BY CHAIRPERSON OF EDUCATION) So much of our time together as Christian educators and church school teachers is spent in workshops or training sessions. It is seldom that we get together to celebrate our lives as Christian educators. Yet what a glorious occupation to celebrate! This is indeed a special day to celebrate. We welcome you and honor you, our teachers.

GRACE: (MINISTER)

HYMN: "I Love to Tell the Story" (THE METHODIST HYMNAL, NO. 149)

Pass On the Story* — A Participation Celebration

LEADER: One of our most important jobs as Christian educators is passing on the stories of our faith. One hundred and fifty-seven times the word "remember" is used in the Bible. Let's listen to some of these admonitions now.

READER 1: Remember then what you were taught and what you heard. (Revelation 3:3)

READER 2: Think of the past, of the time long ago. Ask your fathers to tell you what happened. Ask the old men to tell of the past. (Deuteronomy 32:7)

READER 3: Remember Jesus Christ, who was raised from death, who was a descendant of David, as is taught in the Good News I preach. (2 Timothy 2:8)

READER 4: Remember your servants Abraham, Isaac and Jacob. (Exodus 32:13)

READER 5: I remember the days gone by. I think about all that God has done. I bring to mind all His deeds. (Psalms 143:5)

READER 6: When your son asks who you are, tell him: My father was a wandering Armean whom God called forth. (FROM AN ANCIENT ISRAELITE CREED)

LEADER: We are told to remember — remember our ancestors in the faith — remember our tribulations and victories — remember our unfolding story.

Anyone in the church who hopes to pass the faith along must master the great central stories of the Bible and tell them well. These stories summarize our common heritage. They tell us who we are. They are not just to be read or studied but to be believed, savored and internalized. Each generation must link the past with the present through making these stories their own. And a great responsibility for passing these stories along rests with us, Christian educators and teachers. As an act of worship, now, let's remember our stories.

(LEADER PASSES OUT ELEVEN CARDS WITH STORIES ON THEM)

Anyone who wishes to stand and read may take a card. The cards are numbered. We will read in order. At the end of each reading, let's affirm this story together by singing the last phrase of the chorus of "Blessed Assurance." **"This is my story. This is my song. Praising my Saviour all the day long."** (THE METHODIST HYMNAL, NO. 224)

* *A version of this program appeared in* **The Church School,** *June, 1980, copyrighted by Graded Press. Used by permission.*

CARD 1: Our story begins when there was nothing. Long, long ago before there was anything. But God was there and he created the Heavens and the Earth. He created growing things and living things and then . . . a creature who was made in the very image of God himself. Who had a mind that could wonder about God and a heart that could open to love God.

(ALL SING PHRASE)

CARD 2: Once upon a time there was a man named Abraham, a wandering nomad. God called him forth to be the Father of a special people, the people of God.

(ALL SING PHRASE)

CARD 3: We remember Joseph who stayed true to God in a strange land and used his talents and saved his people from starvation.

(ALL SING PHRASE)

CARD 4: Once upon a time there was a man named Moses. He was raised in a palace, yet destined to rescue the special people of God from slavery. After miracles and marvels he delivered the people from Egypt on the night of the first Passover.

(ALL SING PHRASE)

CARD 5: We remember the stories of Gideon and Ehud and Samson and Saul. When they remained pure and faithful to the spirit of Moses, they prospered. When they gave way to greed, the instinct to survive by power and deceit, they went under.

(ALL SING PHRASE)

CARD 6: We remember David and years of great glory and prosperity when the special people became a nation.

(ALL SING PHRASE)

CARD 7: There was once a prophet called Amos who called the people from disobedience to their God. We remember the message of Amos: "Let justice roll down like water and righteousness as a mighty stream."

(ALL SING PHRASE)

CARD 8: And hear now again the central story of our faith. Once a young Jewish man loved his people and lived their life. He tried to help them fulfill their hopes and dreams by turning their thoughts continually to God and to his love. When he was executed on suspicion of fermenting political upheaval, he died bravely with forgiveness on his lips. He lived in total fidelity and obedience to God, showing others what God plans for man to be and he was raised from the dead.

(ALL SING PHRASE)

CARD 9: We remember the story of Pentecost when amid tongues of fire and swirling of winds a frightened, shattered people became the community of believers and the Christian church began.

(ALL SING PHRASE)

CARD 10: We remember the vivid and gripping stories of Paul; his journeys, his shipwrecks, his imprisonment and his conviction that the only Jesus there is, is Jesus Christ, Lord, Redeemer, Savior — with us now.

(ALL SING PHRASE)

CARD 11: We remember the strange, visionary stories in Revelation in which John proclaims the conviction that we will be telling our stories still when that day comes when all tears will be wiped from our eyes and we shall behold him as he is.

(ALL SING PHRASE)

Sharing

LEADER: Thank you for recalling for us again some of our great stories. And now the torch is passed to you, the teachers and Christian educators. Where would you be if no one had ever told you the stories of our faith? Where will the next generation be if the stories stop with you and are never passed on? Will some of you here recall and share with us where you first heard the stories of our faith? From whom do you remember learning about our Christian faith? In what setting?

(SHARING BY 3 OR 4 TEACHERS)

Thank you for sharing your memories with us.

HYMN: "Tell Me the Stories of Jesus" (THE METHODIST HYMNAL, NO. 88)

MINISTER: (EXPRESSION OF APPRECIATION)

(GROUP FORMS A CIRCLE AND SINGS SUGGESTED SONG)

SONG: "Pass It On" (FROM **TELL IT LIKE IT IS**, LEXICON MUSIC, INC.)

MINISTER: (BENEDICTION) Go forth now as storytellers, telling the stories of our faith to all who will hear.

"Celebrate Our Children" * — a Church-Wide Potluck Supper

INTRODUCTION

Families or other intergenerational groupings sit together around tables. A church-wide supper may precede the celebration or you may wish to end the celebration with refreshments.

PARTICIPANTS

Leader
Children Readers
Adult/Youth Readers
Storyteller
Older Adult
Younger Adult
Youth
Child

MATERIALS

copies of questions and responses

pencils, paper

poster board: black, red, orange, light blue, light lavender, spring green, silver, brown, yellow,
     deep blue, deep purple

yarn

2 one-eighth inch dowels per person

potluck supper or refreshments

SOURCES FOR MUSIC SUGGESTIONS

"Tell Me the Stories of Jesus" — the Methodist Hymnal, No. 88.

"Love Is a Circle" — **Rejoice and Sing Praise,** compiled by Evelyn Andre and Jeneil Menefee,
     Abingdon Press, 1977.

"We Are the Church" — by Avery and Marsh, in **Rejoice and Sing Praise,** (see above).

* A version of this program appeared in **The Church School,** *August, 1980, copyrighted by Graded Press. Used by permission.*

17

CELEBRATION PROGRAM

LEADER: We have come together tonight to celebrate children and the unique contribution that children make to the community of faith. Children are our hopes for the future, children are our most precious possession in the present. We minister to children and they minister to us.

Tonight we welcome the children of our church community with affection and love. Jesus said we are the children of God. Tonight we want to celebrate the child in all of us.

We know that children ask questions. This is part of the growing, learning process. So our program tonight is built around four questions, questions that I am sure every child here has asked. Notice the sheet of paper in front of you. Children, will you please ask Question 1, and adults, will you please give the response?

Games

CHILDREN: (QUESTION 1) Will you play with us?

ADULTS AND YOUTH: Yes. We will play with you because the church is a caring community. We enjoy your laughter and playfulness. We welcome you as a valued person in this congregation.

(THE GROUP NOW PLAYS ONE OR TWO OF THE FOLLOWING SUGGESTED GAMES TOGETHER)

1. SIMON SAYS — The players stand at their places at the table. A leader stands in the center and says, "Simon says, thumbs up." (ANY OTHER MOVEMENT MAY BE GIVEN). At the same time he or she goes through the movement announced, and the other players follow. If the leader performs the act and says merely, "Thumbs up," and omits "Simon says," the players should not follow. Any one who does so must drop out of the game and be seated.

2. DRAW A PROVERB — Each table is a team. Each team chooses a runner who has paper and a pencil. All runners meet with the leader in the center of the room. They are assigned a proverb to draw. They go back to their teams. The runners must not speak, but draw the proverb for their team to guess. The first team guessing correctly wins. Then another runner is chosen and receives a new proverb. Some proverbs are:

>The early bird catches the worm.
>Birds of a feather flock together.
>You can't have your cake and eat it too.
>People who live in glass houses shouldn't throw stones.
>Laugh and the world laughs with you. Cry and you cry alone.
>A stitch in time saves nine.
>Every cloud has a silver lining.
>A penny saved is a penny earned.
>A watched pot never boils.
>A rolling stone gathers no moss.
>An apple a day keeps the doctor away.

3. ACTING OUT NURSERY RHYMES — As in "Draw a Proverb," each table chooses someone as a runner to meet with the leader. Here he or she is given the name of a nursery rhyme. The persons chosen as the runners go back to their tables and act out, without words, the nursery rhyme. Everyone at the table tries to guess what it is. The first table to guess correctly wins. Some nursery rhymes are: Little Jack Horner, Little Miss Muffet, Jack and Jill and Humpty Dumpty.

Story

CHILDREN: (QUESTION 2) Will you tell us a story?

ADULTS AND YOUTH: Yes. We will tell you a story because we have a wonderful story to tell. We long to share with you our exciting heritage. We want to pass on to you the stories of our faith that hold great meaning for us. We appreciate your eagerness to learn and desire to grow.

(FOLLOWING THIS, A STORYTELLER COMES FORWARD AND PRESENTS THE STORY OF CREATION USING LARGE POSTER BOARDS OF VARIOUS COLORS)

STORYTELLER: (HOLDS UP BLACK POSTER BOARD) Our story begins when there was nothing . . . long, long ago before there was anything. Can you imagine Nothing? Think of vast stretches of emptiness. Nothing. But God was there. Before there was Anything. God was there. And God imagined a world.

(HOLDS UP RED POSTER BOARD)

Bright color flashed forth. Worlds and worlds and worlds and motion going round and round and sounds loud and soft. Color exploded. Everything was spinning and twirling and swirling. And God said, "Good!"

(HOLDS UP ORANGE POSTER BOARD)

And God thought, "Let the motion and the color and the sounds make patterns." And it happened! The spinning motion, the color and the sound became worlds. And among the patterns — the endless magnitude of worlds — was one tiny, little speck.

(HOLDS UP LIGHT BLUE POSTER BOARD)

God pondered this tiny world. He loved it. And he imagined blue sky and fluffy white clouds and rain that fell gently.

(HOLDS UP LIGHT LAVENDER POSTER BOARD)

And God imagined mountains stretching high to the blue sky. He imagined a sea going round the land. And earth was beautiful. And God thought, "Let there be something growing on this beautiful earth."

(HOLDS UP SPRING GREEN POSTER BOARD)

And God, who created the mountains so steep and high and the oceans so powerful and massive, caused a tiny thing to grow. God looked at the small growing thing — the green, growing thing — and stem, leaf, bush and tree appeared. Soft green petals uncurled and grew. Fuzzy, green grass pushed up from the earth. And creeping things appeared.

(HOLDS UP SILVER POSTER BOARD)

Fins of swimming things flashed in the cool deep waters. Bright wings fluttered in the sky. And it happened! Life was everywhere.

(HOLDS UP BROWN POSTER BOARD)

Tiny creatures hopped about on the earth. Bold, fierce animals stalked the land. God's thoughts went on and on. The creations of God are beyond our imaginings. Tiny insects with perfectly formed features, birds in every color with intricate wings and different songs. Funny animals like giraffes and flamingoes and kangaroos. God created and created and created!

(FLIP THROUGH A RAINBOW OF COLORS)

But there was something greater that God had in mind.

(HOLDS UP YELLOW POSTER BOARD)

A creature like God himself. One who would care for all the rest. One who had a mind that could wonder about God's plan and a heart that could open to love God. And God thought of people — men and women, boys and girls. And people — in a rainbow of colors — were everywhere.

(HOLDS UP DEEP BLUE POSTER BOARD)

And here we are — God's people all over the earth. And here is the world God planned for us all.

(HOLDS UP DEEP PURPLE POSTER BOARD)

Beyond our world is much more that God planned. And God's thoughts are still going on with many wonders and creations. More than you or I can know, for God's thoughts are very great thoughts. Always there is God. Now, at this very moment, God stretches out forever. Always — there is God.

Song

CHILDREN: (QUESTION 3) Will you sing a song with us?

ADULTS AND YOUTH: Yes. We will sing with you because we want to join with you in praising God. We want to share the joy of worshiping this way together.

(FOLLOWING THIS, THE GROUP SINGS TOGETHER. YOU MAY WISH TO HAVE A SONG LEADER, AND CHOOSE FROM THE FOLLOWING SONGS)

"Tell Me the Stories of Jesus" — (THE METHODIST HYMNAL, NO. 88)

"Love Is a Circle" — (**REJOICE AND SING PRAISE**, ABINGDON PRESS, 1977)

Gifts

CHILDREN: (QUESTION 4) Do you have gifts for us?

ADULTS AND YOUTH: Yes. Because we love to share with you. We appreciate the easy joy you find in little things. And because you love to create, we will all make the gifts together.

LEADER: We are all going to make objects called Ojo de Dios which means the Eye of God. This ancient folk art is still used today by the Heuchol Indians of Mexico in religious festivals.

OJO DE DIOS— (INSTRUCTIONS) Have materials for each table: yarn scraps in a variety of colors, and one-eighth inch dowels, cut in various sizes, but two of the same size for each person. Have instructors who can go around to each table and help with the construction.

Form a cross with your dowel sticks. Lay one end of yarn over the center. Hold the sticks together with your thumb and index finger of your left hand, trapping the yarn with your thumb.

Criss-cross the yarn over the center from right to left until it is covered. Knot the yarn at the back. Keep going around each dowel in order. Pull the yarn tightly as you wrap it. As you start going around the cross again, make sure that each length of yarn is right next to the one from the previous round. Don't overlap the wrappings or the lengths of yarn. Continue in the same way until you are nearly at the end of the dowels. Knot the yarn around the sticks and cut it off neatly. Use as many colors in your God's Eye as you want. To start a new color just cut the old color off and tie the new color onto the end of the old color with a double knot. When everyone has finished, persons at the tables will exchange with each other.

LEADER: When you look at your Eye of God, I hope each of you will remember four other gifts that the people in this church would like to exchange.

(FOUR INDIVIDUALS STAND AND SPEAK)

OLDER ADULT: When you look at the Eye of God, think about Security. God is always watching over us to love us and keep us safe.

YOUNGER ADULT: When you look at the Eye of God, think about Significance. We are very special and important to God.

YOUTH: When you look at the Eye of God, think about Acceptance. God accepts every one of us just as we are.

CHILD: When you look at the Eye of God, think about Love. God loves each of us very much. And so do we in the church.

(ALL JOIN HANDS TOGETHER AROUND THE ROOM AND SING VERSE SIX OF THE FOLLOWING SUGGESTED SONG)

HYMN: "We Are the Church" (REJOICE AND SING PRAISE, ABINGDON PRESS, 1977)

(NOTE: One of the ways we can minister to children outside our congregation is through the program of UNICEF, United Nations' Childrens Emergency Fund. If you wish to include this ministry as part of this program, more information on UNICEF may be secured from: United Nations Committee for UNICEF, 331 East 38th St., New York, N.Y. 10016)

A Children's Thanksgiving Liturgy

INTRODUCTION

One of the oldest Christian hymns is "Jubilatee." Tradition says that early Christians meeting in the catacombs sang this hymn. Tradition also says that as these early Christians walked through the long, dark corridors of the catacombs, singing this song, they moved in a pattern of three steps forward and one step back in rhythm with the music. This ancient procession was called the Tripudium. The procession of children in this service is based on the Tripudium.

PARTICIPANTS

Leader
26 children
Ushers
Minister
Choir

MATERIALS

choir robes
26 sheets of construction paper with letters of the alphabet
sheets of paper and pencils in pews
collection plates
*slides
*slide projector and screen
(*or pictures can be drawn on art or construction paper)

SOURCES FOR MUSIC SUGGESTIONS

"Jubilatee" — in chorus of "Now on Land and Sea Descending," the Methodist Hymnal, No. 505.
"O For a Thousand Tongues to Sing" — the Methodist Hymnal, No. 1.
"Doxology" also called "Praise God from Whom All Blessings Flow" — found in most hymnals
"How Great Thou Art" — the Methodist Hymnal, No. 17.
"We Thy People Praise Thee" — the Methodist Hymnal, No. 6.

PREPARATION

Twenty six slides made by the children may be used in the Psalm meditation in this liturgy. Write-on slides are available at most photographic supply stores or church supply houses. These are blank slides which the children can draw on with black or colored pencils. Any elementary age child can do this. Gather the class together and assign each child a portion of the Scripture to illustrate in any way he or she likes. The Scripture used here, Psalms 104, is full of word pictures. It might be helpful if the children practice first on scrap paper, drawing to the small slide scale. These slides are then projected in a regular slide projector. If slides are not feasible in your situation, the children can draw on regular art or construction paper. In this case, encourage the children to draw large pictures.

You may wish to have the children practice the Jubilatee procession and the alphabet reading of praise and thanksgiving.

LITURGY

LEADER: Come, let us praise the Lord! Let us sing for joy to God who protects us! Let us come before him with thanksgiving and sing joyful songs of praise. (Psalms 95:1)

Jubilatee Procession

INSTRUCTIONS — Twenty six children or youth in choir robes enter to the ancient hymn tune, "Jubilatee." They march down the aisle in 2's if there is room. If not, they may process separately. Leave plenty of room between pairs, at least six pews.

Begin on right foot, arms raised. All process 3 steps forward, 1 step back. Slowly raise and lower arms: Jubilatee (UP 1, 2, 3, 4), Jubilatee (DOWN 1, 2, 3, 4), Jubilatee (UP 1, 2, 3, 4), Jubilatee (DOWN 1, 2, 3, 4), raising and lowering arms on the words, following the rhythm of the song.

Arm movement is added for dramatic effect, but some children have trouble co-ordinating foot movement, arm movement and singing. Modify this in any way that suits your group: regular procession with singing, or foot and arm movement by some as others sing, etc.

(CHOIR SHOULD SING STATELY, BUT JOYFULLY, AS IT PROCESSES)

HYMN: "Jubilatee" (THE METHODIST HYMNAL, CHORUS OF NO. 505)

(CHOIR IS SEATED ON FRONT PEWS OR IN CHOIR LOFT)

LEADER: Let us all now join in a joyful song of praise.

HYMN: "O For a Thousand Tongues to Sing" (THE METHODIST HYMNAL, NO. 1)

LEADER: We can never praise God enough. We can never thank Him enough for all His goodness to us. As far as A is from Z, so far does God's goodness extend. Using the alphabet and the Book of Psalms, our choir will lead us in praise and thanksgiving to our God.

Praise and Thanksgiving

(TWENTY SIX CHILDREN AND YOUTH COME FORWARD ONE AT A TIME. EACH HOLDS A SHEET OF COLORED CONSTRUCTION PAPER WITH HIS OR HER LETTER OF THE

ALPHABET WRITTEN ON IT AND READS OR RECITES HIS OR HER SCRIPTURE. THEN
HE OR SHE RETURNS TO HIS OR HER SEAT)

CHILD A: All you that are righteous shout for joy for what the Lord has done. (Psalms 33:1)

CHILD B: But I will sing about your strength. (Psalms 59:16)

CHILD C: Clap your hands for joy, all people. Praise God with loud songs. (Psalms 47:1)

CHILD D: I depend on God alone. I put my trust in him. (Psalms 62:5)

CHILD E: Every morning I will sing aloud of your constant love. (Psalms 59:16)

CHILD F: Find out for yourself how good the Lord is. (Psalms 34:8)
From the East to the West, praise the name of the Lord. (Psalms 113:3)

CHILD G: Give thanks to the Lord with harps. Sing to him with stringed instruments. (Psalms 33:2)

CHILD H: How wonderful are the good things you keep for those who honor you. (Psalms 31:19)

CHILD I: I will always thank the Lord. I will never stop praising him. (Psalms 34:1)

CHILD J: Your deeds bring shouts of joy from one end of the earth to the other. (Psalms 65:8)

CHILD K: You, O Lord, are King forever. (Psalms 102:12)

CHILD L: Let everything that breathes praise the Lord! (Psalms 150:6 Revised Standard Version)

CHILD M: Make a joyful noise unto the Lord all ye lands. (Psalms 100:1 King James Version)

CHILD N: Not one has done what you have done. There is no god like you, O Lord. (Psalms 86:8)

CHILD O: O God, I will offer you what I have promised. I will give you my offerings of thanksgiving. (Psalms 56:12)

CHILD P: Proclaim with me the Lord's greatness, let us praise His name together. (Psalms 34:3)

CHILD Q: Answer me quickly when I call. (Psalms 102:2)

CHILD R: Remember what the Holy One has done and give him thanks. (Psalms 30:4)

CHILD S: Sing praise to God, sing praise to our king. (Psalms 47:6)

CHILD T: The Lord is great and is to be greatly praised. (Psalms 48:1)

CHILD U: Until I went into your temple . . . I did not understand you. (Psalms 73:16)

CHILD V: You answer us by giving us victory and you do wonderful things to save us. (Psalms 65:5)

CHILD W: With all my heart I will say to the Lord, "There is no one like you." (Psalms 35:10)

CHILD X: Your fame extends over all the earth. (Psalms 48:10)

CHILD Y: You are the source of all life and because of your light we see the light. (Psalms 36:9)

CHILD Z: Zion, the mountain of God, is high and beautiful, the city of the great king brings joy to all the world. (Psalms 48:2)

HYMN: (ALL) "Doxology" also called "Praise God from Whom all Blessings Flow" (FOUND IN MOST HYMNALS)

LEADER: Come, let us bow down and worship him, let us kneel before the Lord our maker. (Psalms 95:6)

As our choir led us in thanking God with the alphabet . . . let us use the same vehicle to offer our thanks to God. Using the letters of your name as an impetus to praise, write on the sheet of paper in your pew your thanks to God.

(USHERS COLLECT SHEETS IN OFFERING PLATES AND BRING TO MINISTER. MINISTER RAISES PLATES TO ALTAR AND SAYS)

MINISTER: Our thanks to you can never be captured with words or letters, but accept these our feeble offerings of praise. Amen.

(PLACES OFFERING PLATES ON ALTAR TABLE)

Psalm Meditation
(A SERMON BY THE MINISTER MAY BE SUBSTITUTED HERE FOR THE PSALM MEDITATION WITH SLIDE ILLUSTRATIONS)

MINISTER: Once the ancient mystic, Ruysbroeck, said, "I must rejoice without ceasing although the world shudder at my job." We cannot help but rejoice as we consider the creations of God. The beautiful Psalm 104 is a peon of praise to God our Creator. The children of the church school have prepared a presentation for us illustrating this psalm.

MINISTER OR LEADER: (Psalms 104) Praise the Lord, my soul! O Lord, my God, how great you are! You are clothed with majesty and glory, you cover yourself with light. You spread out the heavens like a tent and built your home on the waters above.

(SLIDE 1) [each slide coincides with sentence below it]

You use the clouds as your chariot and ride on the wings of the wind.

(SLIDE 2)

You use the winds as your messengers and flashes of lightning as your servants.

(SLIDE 3)

You have set the earth firmly on its foundations, and it will never be moved.

(SLIDE 4)

You placed the ocean over it like a robe and the water covered the mountains.

(SLIDE 5)

When you rebuked the waters they fled . . . they . . . they rushed away when they heard your shout of command.

(SLIDE 6)

They flowed over the mountains and into the valleys to the place that you had made for them.

(SLIDE 7)

You set a boundary they can never pass, to keep them from covering the earth again.

(SLIDE 8)

You made springs flow in the valleys and rivers run between the hills.

(SLIDE 9)

They provide water for the wild animals. There the wild donkeys quench their thirst.

(SLIDE 10)

In the trees near by, the birds make their nests and sing.

(SLIDE 11)

From the sky you send rain on the hills and the earth is filled with your blessings.

(SLIDE 12)

You make grass grow for the cattle and plants for men to use.

(SLIDE 13)

So that he can grow his crops and produce wine to make him happy, olive oil to make him cheerful and bread to give him strength.

(SLIDE 14)

The cedars of Lebanon get plenty of rain . . . the Lord's own trees which he planted.

(SLIDE 15)

There the birds build their nests . . . the storks nest in the fir trees.

(SLIDE 16)

The wild goats live in the high mountains and the badgers hide in the cliffs.

(SLIDE 17)

You created the moon to mark the months, the sun knows the time to set.

(SLIDE 18)

You made the night, and in the darkness all the wild animals come out.

(SLIDE 19)

The young lions roar while they hunt, looking for the food that God provides.

(SLIDE 20)

When the sun rises, they go back and lie down in their dens.

(SLIDE 21)

The people go out to do their work and keep working until evening.

(SLIDE 22)

Lord you have made so many things. How wisely you make them all. The earth is filled with your creatures. There is the ocean, large and wide where countless creatures live, large and small alike.

(SLIDE 23)

The ships sail on it and in it plays Leviathan, that sea monster which you made.

(SLIDE 24)

May the glory of the Lord last forever. May the Lord be happy with what he has made.

(SLIDE 25)

He looks at the earth and it trembles . . . he touches the mountains and they pour out smoke.

(SLIDE 26)

I will sing to the Lord all my life. As long as I live I will sing praises to my God. May he be pleased with my song, for my gladness comes from him.

HYMN: "How Great Thou Art" (THE METHODIST HYMNAL, NO. 17)

LEADER: Praise the Lord's glorious name. Bring an offering and come into his Temple. (Psalms 96:8)

OFFERING: (USHERS TAKE UP COLLECTION)

HYMN: "We Thy People Praise Thee" (THE METHODIST HYMNAL, NO. 6)

(CHOIR MAY RECESS OUT TO "JUBILATEE" MARCH)

MINISTER OR LEADER: (BENEDICTION) Remember what the holy God has done and give thanks to Him. Go forth praising God. (Psalms 97:12)

National Bible Week Observance

INTRODUCTION

National Bible Week is an interfaith effort to encourage the reading of the Bible and the application of its truths to the challenges of daily life. It is a special occasion in many churches. How can we observe this day with meaning in the Church School?

A meaningful way is for the youth (and possibly the children, too) to sponsor a Day of Continuous Bible reading. The Saturday before Bible Sunday is usually the best day. This service features a reading of the Bible without ceasing from 8:00 a.m. to 8:00 p.m. as a ceaseless act of praise to God and thanksgiving for His Holy Word.

For this service, you will need 37 readers and 11 musicians. The readers may be all youth and older children, or adults may be included as well.

In addition to the service of reading, you may wish to have Bible booths open during the morning or afternoon hours.

PARTICIPANTS
37 Readers
11 Musicians

MATERIALS
materials as needed for Bible Booths (optional)
fresh drinking water
decorative posters

ACTIVITY

Bible Booths (optional)

1. BIBLE DISPLAY — Ask members of the congregation to bring unusual Bibles for display. Old family Bibles, the largest Bible, the smallest Bible, Bibles in other languages, Bibles with unusual covers. Provide the participants with name stickers to attach to the Bibles until it is time to reclaim them.

2. BOOKSTORE DISPLAY — A local bookstore might have a display of Bibles for sale.

3. BIBLE CRAFTS — Homemade bookmarks and Bible covers made by Church School classes could be put on display.

Decorations

Bible passages could be prominently displayed on posters. Possible choices are:

"My word is like the snow and the rain that comes down from the sky to water the earth. They make the crops grow and provide seed for planting and food to eat." (Isaiah 55:10)

"My word goes forth from my mouth: it shall not return to me empty, but it shall accomplish that which I purpose and prosper in the thing for which I sent it." (Isaiah 55:11 Revised Standard Version)

Bible Reading

1. Each reader will read for 15 minutes. The first reader should begin with Matthew 1. The second reader will take up where the first reader left off, and so on. When Revelation is completed, the reader reads the Book of Psalms. When this is completed, the reader begins again with Matthew 1.

2. Every hour there will be a short interlude of music on the organ or piano for meditation, prayer and dedication.

3. Members of the congregation may enter quietly at any time. They may leave at any time.

4. If no one is present in the congregation, the reader continues to read aloud.

5. Readers must strive for a feeling of reverence and read with expression.

6. Readers read from the pulpit.

7. When it's time for a reader to start, he or she simply walks to the pulpit beside the current reader. He or she is shown the place in the Bible to start, and takes over the reading.

8. Before each reader begins, he or she says the words: "We believe the Bible is a revelation of the Holy. Hear now these words."

9. Readers may plan to read more than once, but not in two consecutive 15 minute periods.

10. Fresh water should be kept on hand for the readers.

11. The reading is to be a continuous praise to God without ceasing. If the reader following should be late, the current reader should continue to read until he or she can be replaced.

Sign Up Sheet for Readers and Musicians

8:00   Opening by Minister

        First Reader _____

8:15   Second Reader _____

8:30   Third Reader _____

8:45   Fourth Reader _____

9:00   First Musician _____

9:15   Fifth Reader _____

9:30   Sixth Reader _____

9:45   Seventh Reader _____

10:00 Second Musician _____

10:15 Eighth Reader _____

10:30 Ninth Reader _____

10:45 Tenth Reader _____

11:00 Third Musician _____

11:15 Eleventh Reader _____

11:30 Twelfth Reader _____

11:45 Thirteenth Reader _____

12:00 Fourth Musician _____

12:15 Fourteenth Reader _____

12:30 Fifteenth Reader _____

12:45 Sixteenth Reader _____

1:00   Fifth Musician _____

1:15   Seventeenth Reader _____

1:30   Eighteenth Reader _____

1:45   Nineteenth Reader _____

2:00   Sixth Musician _____

2:15   Twentieth Reader _____

2:30   Twenty-first Reader _____

2:45   Twenty-second Reader _____

3:00   Seventh Musician _____

3:15   Twenty-third Reader _____

3:30   Twenty-fourth Reader _____

3:45   Twenty-fifth Reader_____

4:00   Eighth Musician _____

4:15   Twenty-sixth Reader _____

4:30   Twenty-seventh Reader _____

4:45   Twenty-eighth Reader _____

5:00   Ninth Musician_____

5:15   Twenty-ninth Reader _____

5:30   Thirtieth Reader _____

5:45   Thirty-first Reader _____

6:00   Tenth Musician_____

6:15   Thirty-second Reader _____

6:30   Thirty-third Reader _____

6:45   Thirty-fourth Reader _____

7:00   Eleventh Musician _____

7:15   Thirty-fifth Reader _____

7:30   Thirty-sixth Reader _____

7:45   Thirty-seventh Reader _____

8:00   Closing of Day by Minister

WINTER
DECEMBER/JANUARY/FEBRUARY

SPECIAL DAYS IN WINTER

Through the short, dark days of Winter the Church School can be bright and glowing with the celebration of Special Days.

No Church School celebration is more meaningful to a child than the celebration of Christmas. Capture the universality of this festival and the excitement of anticipation with an Advent workshop on crafts from many countries. Capture the simplicity and sacredness of the Christmas story with a twilight Christmas Eve service.

And when the excitement of Christmas has died away, proclaim the great message of the Epiphany season; Christ's continuing revelation in the world today, with a colorful, fun-filled Mission's celebration, and an evening of drama stressing human relations.

Then, in the unfolding sequence of the Church year, begin to prepare the children of the Church School for the next great jubilee occasion, Easter, with a "40-Days" program as an after school event for the beginning of Lent. Here the children get in touch with their own wilderness wanderings as they prepare for the new life of Easter. They learn that the wilderness is also the place where people make covenant with God.

Advent Festival for Children

INTRODUCTION

This is an activity for children, ages 4 to 12, to learn a Christmas custom from another culture.

PARTICIPANTS

Children

Eight teenage or adult leaders

MATERIALS

eight tables

red and green cloths

signs

supplies as listed for each center

PREPARATION

The setting should be a Fellowship Hall with a nearby kitchen. The hall should be set up with eight tables, or "centers," covered with red and green paper cloths. Set eight chairs at each table. A sign on each table should tell what craft will be done there, and its country of origin. An adult or teenage leader should be at each table to explain the instructions and help the children.

Children can gather in a room near the Fellowship Hall for singing of Christmas carols. When all have arrived, take the children on a walking tour of the Fellowship Hall and kitchen as each center is briefly explained. The children can then choose the center in which they wish to work.

Generally, follow these guidelines,

1. Not more than eight children should be at any one center at any time.
2. If a child finishes the craft at one center, he or she may move to another center if there is an opening at that table.
3. Everything the children make is theirs to take home.
4. (optional) You might wish to use the ornaments to decorate a Sunday School room or Christmas Tree.

CRAFT IDEAS*

Center 1 — Drinking-Straw Stars from Sweden

SUPPLIES — drinking straws, red thread

INSTRUCTIONS —

1. Tie 10 drinking straws together at the center. Tie 10 more in the same manner. Tie the two bundles together so you have 20 straws.

2. One inch from the center, tie the straws together in groups of four, using red thread and tying a tight knot. There will be five ties on each side of the center, ten ties in all.

3. Now take two of the four straws from a group and tie to two of an adjoining group at the outer end of the straws. This will form a ten-pointed star.

Center 2 — Gum Drop Bells from England

SUPPLIES — gum drops of all colors, small Christmas bell, needle and thread

INSTRUCTIONS —

1. Thread needle and tie Christmas bell to end of the thread.

2. String eight gum drops above the bell, arranging colors attractively.

3. Tie large knot at top and make a small loop for hanging. Put a wire ornament hook through the loop and hang the gum drop bell vertically on a Christmas tree.

Center 3 — Pomander Balls from Pioneer America

SUPPLIES — medium sized apple, whole cloves, cinnamon, bag, yarn

INSTRUCTIONS —

1. Beginning at top of the apple, press the stems of cloves into apple until it is thickly covered.

2. Place the clove-studded apple in a paper or plastic bag with a small quantity of powdered cinnamon and shake gently until well covered.

3. Tie yarn around the ball and hang on a Christmas tree.

Center 4 — Velvet Covered Balls from Russia

SUPPLIES — styrofoam balls, velvet ribbon, sequins and braid, 6" pipe cleaners

INSTRUCTIONS —

1. Cut six pieces of velvet ribbon on the bias. A 5" ball needs a 7" length of ribbon.

2. Starting from the center of the ball and stretching to the top and bottom, attach the velvet ribbon to the styrofoam ball with pins along edges of material. Overlap edges and continue applying ribbon pieces until the ball is covered.

3. Insert 6" pipe cleaner firmly into the top of the ball as a hanger.

4. Cover pinned seams with bands of trimming.

*See note on page 38.

Center 5 — Flat Paper Chain from Poland

SUPPLIES — colored construction paper, glue, pencil

INSTRUCTIONS —

1. Make links by cutting strips of paper, or by cutting a shape of your own choice.

2. If making a chain of shapes, be sure to cut shapes double with a connecting fold across the top edge.

3. Then link the pieces together and glue, or join the ends of the paper strips with a little glue.

4. Paper chains can be made with links of many colors, sizes or shapes.

Center 6 — Candles and Petticoats from Moravian Church

SUPPLIES — natural beeswax candles (6" high), red crepe paper, tiny straight pins

INSTRUCTIONS —

1. Cut strips of red crepe paper, 3½" by 12".

2. Fold each strip lengthwise and cut a fringe to within ½" of the edge, cutting on folded edge.

3. Leaving the strip folded, wrap the lower half of a candle, starting in the middle and working down, fringe side up. Fasten ends with tiny straight pins.

Center 7 — Wooden Angels from Sweden

SUPPLIES — wooden clothespins, gold or silver paper, gold or silver braid, paint, nail, foil paper

INSTRUCTIONS —

1. Paint wooden clothespin a light color, golden yellow or sky blue. Make a face on rounded edge of clothespin head.

2. Make a crown of gold or silver braid. A ½" braid with loops at the edge makes a nice crown.

3. Cut wings of foil paper, 2" from tip to tip and wide enough to extend 1" on each side of the body. Attach to center back, ½" below the neck.

4. Hang by small wire attached to nail in the top of the head.

Center 8 — Advent Wreath from Germany

SUPPLIES — styrofoam ring, 4 purple candles for each wreath, evergreens

INSTRUCTIONS —

1. Make small hole for candles in the styrofoam ring.

2. Cut evergreens into six to eight inch lengths. With wire, attach greens to base by wrapping wire around ring, catching bunches of greens as you go.

Center 9 — Decorative Cookies from Finland

SUPPLIES — sugar cookies in circles, some solid and some doughnut shaped, icing in red and blue for decorating

INSTRUCTIONS —

Children decorate cookies in any manner they wish with red and blue icing.

* *From* **The Trees of Christmas,** *by Edna Metcalfe. Copyright 1969 by Abingdon Press. Used by permission. This is an excellent book to use if you want more world-wide crafts, or crafts with more difficulty, also.*

Christmas Eve Family Service

INTRODUCTION

This is an informal, candlelight Christmas Eve service for all ages.

PARTICIPANTS

Leader

Minister

Congregation

MATERIALS

Advent candles

cradle

bundle of straw

banners

SOURCES FOR MUSIC SUGGESTIONS

"Silent Night" — found in most hymnals

"Away in a Manger" — found in most hymnals

"Joseph, Dearest Joseph Mine" — **A Book of Christmas Carols,** selected by Haig and Regina
    Shekerjian, Harper and Rowe, 1963.

"Little Jesus Sweetly Sleep" — **A Book of Christmas Carols,** see above.

"Come Into My Heart, Lord Jesus" — found in **Action Songs for Boys and Girls,** Singspiration
    Series, Zondervan Publishing House.

"O Holy Night" — found in most hymnals

"Joy to the World" — found in most hymnals

PREPARATION

INSTRUCTIONS FOR BANNERS — Parents of children baptized during the year should meet at least several weeks before this program. At this meeting, each set of parents will be given a large piece of felt. All pieces of felt should be of similar size for the basic banner. Scraps of felt in all colors and books of Christian symbols should also be available. The parents will be instructed to put their child's name and birth date on the banner and decorate it with any Christian symbol(s) they desire.

For example, a shell could be used to symbolize Christian baptism. Others could be used to symbolize wishes parents have for their child, such as a musical note to symbolize the wish for music in the child's life. Be careful not to give too much instruction as to design, because the beauty of these banners is in their originality and creativity.

As the banners are presented on Christmas Eve, be sure to read the name of the child. Children who were baptized early in the year may recognize their name being called by the Minister and if so, their response is delightful. It is also nice if these banners can be hung or displayed in some way in the church during the entire Epiphany season, then given to the parents to keep.

ORDER OF SERVICE

Call to Worship
Lighting of Advent Candles
Carol: "Silent Night"
Scripture: Luke 2:1-7
Cradle Rocking Experience
Deeds of Love
Congregational Prayer
Song: "Come Into My Heart, Lord Jesus"
Responsive Sentences
Solo: "O Holy Night"
Scripture: Luke 2:22-38
New Parents Present Banners
Congregational Response
Carol: "Joy to the World"

LITURGY

MINISTER: (CALL TO WORSHIP) Tonight is Christmas Eve. It is time to pause now. It is time to relax from all the excitement of getting ready for Christmas. It is time to sit down together and tell the story. It is time to wonder about this awesome event. Pause now and wonder.

LIGHT ADVENT CANDLES

CAROL: "Silent Night" (FOUND IN MOST HYMNALS)

SCRIPTURE: Luke 2:1-7

Cradle Rocking Experience

LEADER: Our story is a very simple story, the birth of a baby. There was a loving mother and father and a cradle. Sense the wonder in this simple scene as we sing:

HYMN: "Away in a Manger" (FOUND IN MOST HYMNALS)

LEADER: (contd) Come forward and join in rocking the cradle and lulling the baby to sleep.

(OTHER LULLABY CAROLS MAY BE SUNG AS A SOLO OR ANTHEM AS THE CONGREGATION COMES FORWARD. FOR EXAMPLE, "JOSEPH, DEAREST JOSEPH MINE," OR "LITTLE JESUS SWEETLY SLEEP," BOTH FROM **A BOOK OF CHRISTMAS CAROLS**, HARPER AND ROWE, 1963)

(PERSONS COME BY PEWS. WITH HELP OF MINISTER THEY GENTLY ROCK THE CRADLE AND RETURN TO THEIR SEATS. CONTINUE SINGING UNTIL ALL HAVE HAD AN EXPERIENCE OF CRADLE ROCKING)

Deeds of Love

MINISTER: Our crib has no baby in it. Jesus is not being born in a crib tonight. He is being born in us. Jesus is born in the world every time we do kind acts for others.

I have a bundle of straw here beside me. Let this straw be a symbol of a kind act you could do or have done to get ready for the coming of Jesus. Search your hearts now. What kind act have you done or could you still do to get ready for Christmas? When you think of something, come forward. Tell us your deed and take a straw. Put it in the manger. It will really fill our manger if everyone thinks of an act he did or could do.

(CONGREGATION RESPONDS SPONTANEOUSLY, THEN RETURNS TO SEATS)

PRAYER IN UNISON: And now comes Christmas. Now comes the Christ child again. May we mirror his light. May we share his life. May we return his love. Come into our hearts, Lord Jesus.

(SING TOGETHER THE FOLLOWING REFRAIN. "COME INTO OUR HEARTS, LORD JESUS" FOUND IN **ACTION SONGS FOR BOYS AND GIRLS**, SINGSPIRATION SERIES, ZONDERVAN PUBLISHING HOUSE)

*REFRAIN: Into my heart, Into my heart,
Come into my heart, Lord Jesus.
Come in today, Come in to stay,
Come into my heart, Lord Jesus.

Out of my heart, Out of my heart,
Shine out of my heart, Lord Jesus.
Shine out today, Shine out always,
Shine out of my heart, Lord Jesus.

*"Come Into My Heart, Lord Jesus" copyright 1924, renewal 1952 by Hope Publishing Co. Words used by special permission.

Responsive Sentences

MINISTER: Christmas is always full of gifts and surprises. But the biggest surprise of all was that Jesus, the long-awaited Saviour, came as a tiny baby and he was born in a poor place like a stable.

CONGREGATION: Who would have ever thought that?

MINISTER: And Jesus was the best gift of all, too. A gift from God to us, to tell us what God is like, how to live our lives, to bring us life forever.

CONGREGATION: Who would have ever thought of that?

MINISTER AND CONGREGATION: We thank you, Lord Jesus, for being the biggest surprise and best gift of all. Unto us a child is born.

MINISTER: Let us pause and wonder about this surprise . . . about this gift.

SOLO: "O Holy Night" (FOUND IN MOST HYMNALS)

MINISTER: When Jesus was 40 days old, he was presented at the Temple, as was the custom. Let's listen to this story as it is recorded in our Scripture: Luke 2:22-38. (READ)

New Parents Present Banners

MINISTER: This year in our church we have also presented children to God. Here with us tonight are the children who have been baptized this year. Their parents, loving them, as Mary and Joseph loved their son, have created banners of hopes and wishes for their children.

Will these parents come forward now and share their banners with us?

(PARENTS COME FORWARD AND EXPLAIN AND PRESENT THEIR BANNERS. AS EACH BANNER IS PRESENTED, THE CONGREGATION RESPONDS WITH)

CONGREGATION: May the hope, love and joy of Christmas ever accompany this child.

MINISTER: (BENEDICTION) Christ is born into our lives each time we experience that sense of birth that brings us joy and a sense of Christ's presence.

CAROL: "Joy to the World" (FOUND IN MOST HYMNALS)

Let's Be Friends — Mission Celebration

INTRODUCTION

This is a joyful celebration to affirm that living in covenant with God means caring about all of God's children as God cares about us. This can be celebrated intergenerationally or for all children in the elementary Church School.

PARTICIPANTS

Program Leader
Leaders for each corner
Four Student Readers
Children

MATERIALS

crepe paper streamers, inflatable globe
construction paper, (extra sheets of red)
butcher paper
fabric, wallpaper
jewelry
felt-tipped pens, scissors, glue
books of costumes
ball of yarn
refreshments

SOURCES FOR MUSIC SUGGESTIONS

"He's Got the Whole World in His Hand" — **The Good Times Songbook,** James Leisy,
    Abingdon Press, 1974.
"Let There Be Peace on Earth" — **Rejoice and Sing Praise,** compiled by Evelyn Andre and Jeneil
    Menefee, Abingdon Press, 1977.
"Kum Ba Yah" — **The Good Times Songbook,** see above.
"It's a Small World" — available in sheet music form at most local music stores.
"Jesus Loves the Little Children" — **Action Songs for Boys and Girls,** Singspiration Series,
    Zondervan Publishing House.

PREPARATION

The setting for this celebration should be a large Fellowship hall. Decorate the entire room with streamers of multi-colored crepe paper draped from a center point in the room to all sides of the hall. Get a large inflatable globe of the world and suspend it at the center point. Leave the walls bare. They will be covered as part of the program. Directly under the globe, leave a space for the program leader. On the floor, place pieces of red construction paper taped to the floor surrounding the center area in a circular pattern.

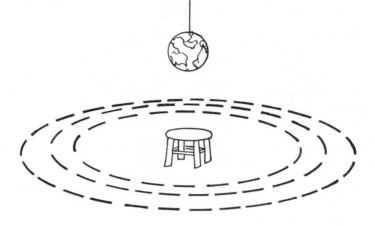

At each corner of the room, set up supplies to learn about different countries and lands. Africa, the Orient, the Middle East and South America are suggested. You may use different countries or lands if they are more appropriate to your studies. Supplies should include: large pieces of butcher paper, pieces of fabric, wallpaper, construction paper, jewelry, felt-tipped pens, scissors, glue and books of costumes for the particular land covered in that corner.

PROGRAM

As children enter, they are told to sit on the red squares. These are magic carpets that will fly them around the world.

LEADER: Welcome boys and girls! How many of you like secrets? We have come together tonight to share with you a secret and to have fun celebrating that secret. We will read from a letter written by St. Paul to his friends at Ephesus. It is found in our Bible and says this: "In past time men were not told this secret, but God has revealed it now by the Spirit to his holy apostles and prophets. The secret is this: (PARAPHRASED) Jesus came to teach us to love everyone with all our hearts and minds and souls. But he didn't come to give this secret of life to just a few chosen friends. He wanted everyone all over the earth to learn this secret. He wanted people from every nation on earth to love one another."

We are so glad that God has told us this and we want to celebrate it together. Let's join now in singing some songs together about this wonderful secret.

(SONG LEADER MAY LEAD GROUP IN SUCH SONGS AS ARE LISTED HERE)

"He's Got the Whole World in His Hand" (**GOOD TIMES SONGBOOK**, ABINGDON PRESS)

"Let There Be Peace On Earth" (**REJOICE AND SING PRAISE**, ABINGDON PRESS)

"Kum Ba Yah" (**THE GOOD TIMES SONGBOOK**, ABINGDON PRESS)

"It's a Small World" (AVAILABLE IN SHEET MUSIC FORM FROM LOCAL MUSIC STORES)

"Jesus Loves the Little Children" (**ACTION SONGS FOR BOYS AND GIRLS**, ZONDERVAN PUBLISHING CO., SINGSPIRATION SERIES)

LEADER: Now, in our imaginations we are going to "meet" some other children from around the world. Imagine the red paper you are sitting on as your own magic carpet. It is going to fly you away to another land. (THE LEADER SHOULD DEVELOP THIS IDEA FURTHER, COMMENTING ON CLOUDS, ETC.)

We have now arrived in Africa. All the children sitting on my right will now get off their magic carpets and go with their leader to the far corner of the room to explore this land. (THESE CHILDREN DO SO WITH THEIR LEADER)

The rest of us will continue to fly. (IMAGINATIVE COMMENTS BY LEADER)

Now we have arrived in the Orient. All the children on my left will leave their magic carpets here and go with their leader to explore this land. (THESE CHILDREN GO TO ANOTHER CORNER WITH A LEADER)

Where will our magic carpets take us next? Ah, here we are in the Middle East. Look at the camels and palm trees. The children in front of me will get off their magic carpets here and go to explore this land. (THESE CHILDREN AND THEIR LEADER GO TO A THIRD CORNER OF THE ROOM)

Well, there are still some of us left. We will fly and fly. Look below. Where could we be? It looks like — yes, it is — South America! Everyone, off your carpets now and we will explore this land together. (CHILDREN AND PROGRAM LEADER GO TO A FOURTH CORNER OF THE ROOM)

Corner Activities

The leader in each area talks with the group about the children of their particular land. Then the children lie down on the butcher paper and have their bodies traced. They then dress these outlines in costumes of the countries they have chosen from the land they are studying. When they have completed these, they cut out the images and mount them on the wall. Place them so that their hands touch, if possible. The room will be surrounded by children from all lands holding hands.

This activity will take some time. It should be fairly free and unstructured so that the children can enjoy the art work of the other areas as well as their own. When this activity is completed, the children are called back to the magic carpet area and instructed to sit on their carpets.

Yarn Picture

LEADER: Boys and girls, we have made and met new imaginary friends. Now we want to learn a Bible verse and hear a story. The Bible verse is this: Proverbs 17:17 — A friend loves at all times. (Revised Standard Version)

(PRACTICE THIS VERSE WITH THE GROUP)

LEADER: (contd) Remember this verse. We will use it later in this program.

The Bible tells us to love our friends and Jesus tells us to love our neighbors. But who is my neighbor anyway? Jesus told a story once that answered this question.

There are many ways to learn a story. We can read it for ourselves or hear it told, or see it on television. Tonight four of our students are going to "weave" us a story. The story which Jesus told answered the question: "Who is my neighbor?" It is the story of the Good Samaritan.

(FOUR STUDENTS COME FORWARD AND SIT ON THE FLOOR IN THE CENTER OF THE MAGIC CARPET AREA. ONE OF THEM IS CARRYING A COLORFUL BALL OF YARN)

STUDENT 1: (BEGINS THE STORY HOLDING THE BALL OF YARN) (Luke 10:30)
A certain man was going down from Jerusalem to Jericho when robbers attacked him.

(AS HE OR SHE FINISHES THIS PORTION, HOLDING ON TO THE LOOSE END OF THE YARN, HE OR SHE THROWS THE BALL OF YARN TO STUDENT 2)

STUDENT 2: Stripped him . . . (THROWS BALL OF YARN TO STUDENT 3)

STUDENT 3: beat him up . . . (THROWS BALL OF YARN TO STUDENT 4)

STUDENT 4: leaving him half dead. (THROWS BALL OF YARN TO STUDENT 1)

STUDENT 1: It so happened that a priest was going down that road, but when he saw the man, he walked on by on the other side.

(TOSSES BALL OF YARN TO STUDENT 3)

STUDENT 3: In the same way a Levite also came there, went over and looked at the man, and then walked on by, on the other side.

(TOSSES YARN TO STUDENT 2)

STUDENT 2: But a certain Samaritan who was traveling that way came upon the man, and when he saw him, his heart was filled with pity.

(TOSSES YARN TO STUDENT 4)

STUDENT 4: He went over to him, poured oil and wine on his wounds and bandaged them.

(TOSSES YARN TO STUDENT 1)

STUDENT 1: Then he put the man on his own animal and took him to an inn, where he took care of him.

(TOSSES YARN TO STUDENT 3)

STUDENT 3: The next day he took out two silver coins and gave them to the innkeeper. "Take care of him," he told the innkeeper. "And when I come back this way I will pay you back whatever else you spent on him."

(TOSSES YARN TO STUDENT 4)

STUDENT 4: Jesus said, "Which one of these three seems to you to have been a neighbor to the man attacked by the robbers?"

(TOSSES YARN TO STUDENT 2)

STUDENT 2: Not the priest! (TOSSES YARN TO STUDENT 1)

STUDENT 1: Not the Levite! (TOSSES YARN TO STUDENT 3)

STUDENT 3: The one who was kind to him. (TOSSES YARN TO STUDENT 4)

STUDENT 4: Jesus replied — You... (TOSSES YARN TO STUDENT 1)

STUDENT 1: go ... (TOSSES YARN TO STUDENT 2)

STUDENT 2: and do ... (TOSSES YARN TO STUDENT 3)

STUDENT 3: the same.

(STUDENTS HOLD UP THEIR YARN PICTURE. TEACHER TAKES THE YARN AND THEY RETURN TO THEIR PLACES IN THE CIRCLE)

LEADER: Will you all stand now and join hands? We are joined in a circle to remind us that we are all one. We are all children of God. We have learned Jesus' secret of life — that we are to love one another and be kind to one another. Will you bow your heads and pray silently for all the children of the world? Then I will close with a prayer and for our benediction, we will say together the Bible verse we learned earlier.

(SILENT PRAYER)

LEADER: (contd) God, please help us to understand one another, to be kind to one another, to trust one another and to see the good in one another. We ask this through Jesus Christ.

ALL: A friend loves at all times. (Proverbs 17:17 Revised Standard Version)

(THE PROGRAM MAY BE FOLLOWED BY REFRESHMENTS)

Mini-Dramas for Human Relations Day

INTRODUCTION

This is a combined Church School program or special evening observance for the Fellowship Hall. The purpose of Human Relations Day is to break down walls of class, wealth and poverty, generations, culture and language as well as barriers between races.

PARTICIPANTS

Master of ceremonies
Cast as indicated for each skit
Narrator (1 or more)

MATERIALS

masks (see Preparation)
animal suits (optional)
props as indicated for each skit
amplification for an offstage voice

SOURCES FOR MUSIC SUGGESTIONS

"He's Got the Whole World in His Hand" — **The Good Times Songbook**, James Leisy, Abingdon
     Press, 1974.
"Blest Be the Tie That Binds" — the Methodist Hymnal, No. 306.

PREPARATION

Animal costumes will consist of large paper plates with animal features drawn on them. Players may wear animal body suits or regular clothing. The plates will be set on top of the players' heads like hats, and held by string or ribbon tied under the chin. Players tuck heads down, causing the paper plate masks to be in face position when players are not speaking. When speaking, players raise their heads so that their voices project. People characters are also designated by hats. Other instructions are given with individual skits.

ORDER OF PROGRAM

Song: "He's Got the Whole World in His Hand"

Fables and Folktales

Skit 1: The Lion and the Mouse

Skit 2: Grandfather's Advice

Skit 3: The Marvelous Pear Tree

Skit 4: The Monkey and the Camel

Skit 5: Mr. Wolf and His Tail

Stories of Jesus

Skit 6: Jesus Meets Bartemaeus

Skit 7: Jesus Meets a Rich, Young Ruler

Skit 8: Jesus Meets the Woman of Sameria

Skit 9: Jesus Meets a Tax Collector

Hymn: "Blest Be the Tie that Binds"

PROGRAM

(SETTING SHOULD BE A STAGE IF POSSIBLE. THE SKITS COULD BE USED AS CHANCEL SKITS IF NECESSARY)

MASTER OF CEREMONIES: (WELCOMES GROUP)

SONG: He's Got the Whole World in His Hand" (**THE GOOD TIMES SONGBOOK**, ABINGDON PRESS, 1974)

MASTER OF CEREMONIES: Labels are good in grocery stores. By means of labels we know which boxes contain rice and which ones detergent. A label tells a can of beans from a can of tomatoes. But labels are not good when they are put on people.

Every human being is a marvelously unique combination of individual characteristics, never before experienced and never again to be repeated. Today (or tonight) is Human Relations Day in our church. A day when we celebrate the uniqueness of all the children of God.

But, back to labels. Have you ever forgotten this uniqueness of each person and stuck a label on a whole group of people, the young — the old — the physically or mentally handicapped — the poor — the rich? You know what I mean. When we start labeling people, we raise or lower the value of our brothers and sisters and we are on the road to the inhumane prejudgment of others.

Fables and Folktales

MASTER OF CEREMONIES: (contd) By means of folktales and fables, we want to illustrate this for you tonight. Our first skit is "The Lion and the Mouse."

SKIT 1: THE LION AND THE MOUSE
(CAST: LION, MOUSE, HUNTER, NARRATOR, ACTION DONE IN PANTOMIME AT START)
(PROPS: HUNTER'S HAT, TOY GUN, ROPE, TREE OPTIONAL)

NARRATOR: Once upon a time there was a great lion.

(LION CHARACTER ENTERS AND CURLS UP ON FLOOR, CENTER STAGE)

The lion had had a very hard morning hunting and roaring.

(LION RAISES HEAD AND ROARS)

And now this great King of the Beasts was very tired.

(LION YAWNS AND STRETCHES)

But just as the lion was beginning to relax in the warm sun, just as his muscles lost their tautness and his eyelids began to droop, up frisked a little mouse.

(MOUSE CHARACTER SKIPS IN)

The mouse was feeling good. Her little body twitched with energy and she was in the mood for fun.

(MOUSE SKIPS ABOUT, SQUEAKING)

She didn't notice the sleeping lion and was soon running up and down upon him.

(MOUSE TIPTOES AND JUMPS OVER LION)

At first the lion tried to ignore her. Then he tried to twitch her off, but still the mouse continued to run and play.

(ACTION ACCOMPANIES WORDS)

Finally the lion lost his patience — jumped up and grabbed the mouse with his huge paws.

(NARRATOR TURNS ATTENTION TO ACTORS, WHO TAKE UP LINES)

LION: Gotcha! And now I will eat you up.

(OPENS MOUTH WIDE)

MOUSE: O, Mister Lion, please, please don't!

LION: Why shouldn't I? Roar. Growl.

MOUSE: Well, you never know. One day I may be able to help you.

LION: You? Help me? That's ridiculous!

MOUSE: No, it isn't. Please, oh please, have mercy. Let me go and I promise to repay the debt.

LION: That's funny! You help me? Oh well, I'm not hungry anyway. Go on.

MOUSE: Oh thank you! Thank you! Squeak! Squeak! I will repay you! I will! You'll see. I will! I will!

(MOUSE SKIPS OFF. LION SHAKES HIS HEAD AND SETTLES BACK TO SLEEP)

NARRATOR: Soon along came a hunter and saw the sleeping lion.

(MAN IN HUNTER'S HAT WITH TOY GUN AND ROPE APPEARS)

HUNTER: Ah, what a fine specimen. Just what I need for my zoo. I'll just shoot him with my tranquilizer gun and tie him to this tree while I go get my wagon to carry him away.

NARRATOR: And the hunter did just that.

(MAN SHOOTS GUN. LION ROLLS OVER WITH FEET IN AIR. MAN PUTS ROPE AROUND HIS NECK AND TIES IT TO A TREE [REAL PROP OR IMAGINARY]. THEN HE LEAVES)

NARRATOR: (contd) Some time later the lion woke up.

LION: Where am I? What happened?

(HE TRIES TO MOVE, BUT CANNOT)

LION: (contd) Help! Help! Somebody help me.

NARRATOR: But who could help the King of the Beasts? Who was mighty enough to break a rope that held his powerful strength?

(LITTLE MOUSE COMES IN AGAIN)

MOUSE: Oh dear! Oh dear! Oh dear!

LION: Go away.

MOUSE: No. No. I can help you. With my little teeth. You'll see.

(MOUSE BEGINS GNAWING AT ROPE. SOON IT BREAKS)

(LION STANDS UP)

MOUSE: You see? I repaid my debt and was I not right? Little friends can sometimes help big friends.

(LION AND MOUSE EXIT ARM-IN-ARM)

NARRATOR: Aesop told that fable many, many years ago reminding us that the young should not be labeled. But neither should the old.
— END OF SKIT 1 —

MASTER OF CEREMONIES: A folktale as old as Aesop's comes to us from Lettish peasants who since time out of mind have been farming the land south of the Gulf of Riga. This then is our next tale: "Grandfather's Advice."

SKIT 2: GRANDFATHER'S ADVICE
(CAST: GRANDFATHER, FATHER, SON, NARRATOR)
(PROPS: TWO PACKING BOXES ARE MOVED INTO PLACE ON EACH SIDE OF THE STAGE. ONE IS DRAWN TO RESEMBLE A FIREPLACE. THE OTHER IS TO RESEMBLE A FOREST OF TREES. A ROCKING CHAIR IS IN FRONT OF THE FIREPLACE AND A SLED LIES BE-SIDE THE FIREPLACE. ALSO NEED — COAT, HAT, WRAPPER)

NARRATOR: Once upon a time people thought everything should be young and new. If some-thing wasn't young and new it was no good. And so when a man got old and could not do his share of work, they had no use for him. It was the custom to get rid of these old folks who were only a burden.

Now at this time there was a man who had an old father and a little son.

(THREE CHARACTERS ENTER. GRANDFATHER SITS IN ROCKING CHAIR)

NARRATOR: (contd) Grandfather was very feeble. Indeed, he scarcely moved from his place by the fire. As was the custom, the son had to get rid of him. So he took his little son's sled and piled the old grandfather onto it.

(MAN PUTS COAT, HAT, WRAPPER ON OLD MAN, LIFTS HIM ONTO SLED)

LITTLE SON: What are you doing with Grandfather?

FATHER: It is the custom.

LITTLE SON: But where are you taking him?

FATHER: It is the custom.

LITTLE SON: Let me come too.

(FATHER SHRUGS, BEGINS PULLING SLED TOWARD FOREST. LITTLE SON HOPS AFTER SLED)

NARRATOR: At last they came to the forest.

(MAN DROPS SLED ROPE, SHRUGS HIS SHOULDERS, SHAKES HIS HEAD AND TURNS TO GO HOME)

NARRATOR: (contd) It was a hard thing to leave old grandfather there in the forest to die, but that was the custom.

LITTLE SON: You mustn't leave Grandfather here in the forest. He will surely die.

FATHER: He is too old to work. It is our custom.

LITTLE SON: But I love him. I will miss him.

(FATHER STARTS BACK TO HOUSE. LITTLE SON STAYS AWHILE WITH GRANDFATHER, THEN RUNS TO CATCH UP WITH FATHER)

LITTLE SON: (contd) Father, father. You mustn't leave my sled there.

FATHER: Why not?

LITTLE SON: Because when you are old and worn out I'll need the sled to carry you to the forest.

(FATHER LOOKS AT SON A LONG TIME)

FATHER: Perhaps I haven't done such a sensible thing. You are right. I was wrong. We'll go and fetch Grandfather home again.

(MAN BRINGS SLED AND GRANDFATHER BACK TO HOUSE. PLACES GRANDFATHER BACK IN ROCKING CHAIR)

NARRATOR: Now that very winter there was a famine in the village and throughout all the land. No one knew what to do. Things got worse and worse. The whole village was starving. Then grandfather spoke:

GRANDFATHER: You and all your neighbors take the old straw off half the roof on your threshing barn and thresh it well.

NARRATOR: They did as he advised. Quite a little grain had been left in the thatch and there was enough grain to survive the long winter.

Grandfather called his son again.

GRANDFATHER: Put back the threshed thatch and take the other half off the roof, thresh that and plant that grain.

NARRATOR: They did as he advised and got a fine crop of rye.

FATHER: But, Father, how did you know?

GRANDFATHER: Once, long ago when I was a boy, we did the same.

FATHER: How fortunate I did not leave you in the forest. We would all have died. We need the wisdom and guidance of age.

(ACTORS EXIT, SCENE IS REMOVED)

— END OF SKIT 2 —

MASTER OF CEREMONIES: Sometimes we don't put people into categories by age, but by their social position. This next folktale, "The Marvelous Pear Tree," comes to us from the people of China.

SKIT 3: THE MARVELOUS PEAR TREE
(CAST: THIEF, POLICEMAN, FRUIT VENDOR, EMPEROR, 4 ATTENDANTS TO THE EMPEROR, NARRATOR; ALL ACTORS WEAR HATS TO DESIGNATE THEIR ROLES)
(PROPS: COSTUME OF RAGS, A PEAR, A PEAR SEED, THRONE OR CHAIR)

NARRATOR: Once upon a time there was a very poor man. Sometimes driven by hunger, he would steal a loaf of bread. When the cold winds blew and whistled through his shabby clothes, he would steal a bit of cloth to wrap around himself. One day he stole a pear.

(THIEF ENTERS DRESSED IN RAGS, LOOKING FURTIVELY TO RIGHT AND LEFT. HE BEGINS EATING A PEAR IN HIS HANDS)

(AN ANGRY FRUIT VENDOR, DRAGGING A POLICEMAN, ENTERS AND POINTS TO THIEF)

NARRATOR: (contd) The poor man thought no one had seen him, but alas they had. He was dragged off to jail and thrown in a dark, dreary cell.

(POLICEMAN GRABS HIM BY COLLAR AND LEADS HIM AWAY, THROWS HIM ON FLOOR AT ONE SIDE OF STAGE, PANTOMIMES LOCKING HIM UP AND TAKES A POSITION IN FRONT OF CELL WITH HANDS FOLDED OVER CHEST. FRUIT VENDOR HAS EXITED OPPOSITE SIDE)

NARRATOR: (contd) Days and then months passed.

(THIEF SITS ON FLOOR WITH HEAD IN HIS HANDS)

NARRATOR: (contd) He was beginning to think his trial would never come up and he would spend the rest of his life in that dark, dank prison cell. All that remained of his terrible crime was one small, brown seed — the last of the pear. Then he had an idea.

51

THIEF: (JUMPING UP) Guard, guard! I want to see the Emperor.

POLICEMAN: Why are you making all this noise?

THIEF: I want to see the Emperor. I have a rare gift for him.

POLICEMAN: A rare gift? I see.

THIEF: Take me to the palace at once.

(A THRONE IS BROUGHT ON STAGE, OPPOSITE FROM JAIL. EMPEROR ENTERS AND SITS ON THRONE. FOUR MEN STAND BESIDE HIM. POLICEMAN AND THIEF APPROACH THRONE AND BOW)

EMPEROR: Are you the one with a rare gift for me?

THIEF: Yes, O Emperor.

EMPEROR: But you are nothing but a ragged beggar. What can you possibly have for me?

THIEF: This, your majesty.

(PULLS OUT PEAR SEED AND HOLDS IT HIGH)

EMPEROR: (TAKES SEED AND LOOKS AT IT) You mean this ordinary pear seed?

THIEF: Ah. This is not an ordinary pear seed. If you will but plant it, it will grow into a marvelous tree which will bear pears of pure gold.

EMPEROR: What a strange story. But if this is true, why did you not plant it and become wealthy?

THIEF: Alas, it would not work for me because you see it will not bear golden fruit unless it is planted by a person who has never stolen anything in his life or cheated anyone, either. That is why I brought it to you, oh great and noble Emperor. Surely you have never stolen anything in your life, or cheated anyone.

NARRATOR: But the Emperor sat in silence. He knew he could not plant the seed. Just last week he had taken over the estate of a nobleman recently beheaded.

(EMPEROR SHAKES HEAD. THIEF HOLDS SEED TO MAN BESIDE THRONE)

THIEF: Then let your Prime Minister plant it.

NARRATOR: But the Prime Minister stood silent. Just last week he had accepted a bribe and there were the court records he had changed to improve his own fortune.

(PRIME MINISTER SHAKES HIS HEAD. THIEF GOES TO NEXT MAN)

THIEF: Here of course, the head of our Army and Navy. This worthy person can plant the seed.

NARRATOR: But the Commander stood silent. Just last week he had kept a horse for himself that was supposed to go to the Royal Stables. And there were the promotions he had sold to the highest bidder.

(COMMANDER SHAKES HIS HEAD. THIEF GOES TO NEXT MAN)

THIEF: The Chief Magistrate then?

NARRATOR: But the Chief Magistrate stood silent. Just last week he had decided a case unfairly.

(CHIEF MAGISTRATE SHAKES HEAD. THIEF GOES TO FOURTH MAN)

THIEF: What about the Chief Warden of the Royal Prison?

NARRATOR: But the Chief Warden stood silent. Just last week he accepted money from a prisoner for better treatment.

(CHIEF WARDEN SHAKES HIS HEAD)

NARRATOR: (contd) So it went, down to the lowest page in the Emperor's court. No one would plant the seed that would produce golden pears.

THIEF: Everyone of you has admitted that he lies, steals and cheats, yet you do not have to go to prison for it. Yet, I, because I stole a pear when I was hungry, I have been cast into prison and forgotten. Would this have happened if I had not been a poor man?

EMPEROR: (SPEAKS AT LAST) What you say is true. Go. You are a free man.

— END OF SKIT 3 —

MASTER OF CEREMONIES: Back to Aesop now. His fables are full of tales of how ridiculous it is for us to expect all people to be alike. This one is about "The Monkey and the Camel."

SKIT 4: THE MONKEY AND THE CAMEL
(CAST: CAMEL, MONKEY, A NUMBER OF VARIOUS OTHER ANIMALS)
(NO PROPS)

NARRATOR: Once upon a time there was a gathering of the animals. A monkey danced with such skill that all the beasts applauded.

(MONKEY COMES TO MIDDLE OF CIRCLE AND DANCES. ANIMALS APPLAUD)

A camel who was watching was jealous. He tried to dance in the same way, but only made a fool of himself and all the animals jeered.

(CAMEL COMES TO MIDDLE OF CIRCLE AND DANCES. ANIMALS JEER)

It's foolish to try to be what you aren't. A camel can't act like a monkey.

(ALL ANIMALS EXIT)

— END OF SKIT 4 —

MASTER OF CEREMONIES: All right now. Good. We have learned that each child of God is unique. We are as rich in diversity as the flowers of the field. Human beings exist in a variety of colors, ages, mental and physical abilities and social status.

But our ability to recognize individuality has at the same time become a tool used to separate us from others. Understanding differences in people makes us at times feel lonely and apart. If we are all different, how will we ever get along?

A strong message from our Christian faith is that though we are all different, we are all necessary to God's plan and Christians have a constant hope that we can indeed be like Jesus and come to love other persons as ourselves. Going again to the world of animal fables, we get this message in the fable of "Mr. Wolf and His Tail."

SKIT 5: MR. WOLF AND HIS TAIL
(CAST: WOLF, WOLF'S EYES, WOLF'S EARS, WOLF'S FEET, WOLF'S TAIL, DOG)
(PROPS: SIGNS AROUND EACH CHARACTER'S NECK, TELLING WHO THEY ARE)

(THROUGHOUT SKIT, FEET HOLDS FOOT EXTENDED, EARS CUPS HANDS OVER EARS, EYES CUPS HANDS OVER EYES AS EYEBROWS, TAIL HAS ARMS RAISED, RESTING ON TOP OF HEAD)

NARRATOR: One day Mr. Wolf went out walking when he was spotted by some big, vicious dogs. They began to chase him. Luckily, Mr. Wolf suddenly saw a cave in the mountain. It was just big enough for him to get inside and he dashed in quickly. The cave was too small for the big dogs, so they waited outside, sniffing and growling.

(WOLF COMES IN AND SPRAWLS ON FLOOR, PANTING. OTHER CHARACTERS COME AND STAND SILENTLY BEHIND HIM)

WOLF: Huh-huh-huh-Wheew! That was close! (CONTINUES PANTING FOR A FEW MOMENTS, THEN STANDS UP AND STRETCHES) Hmmm, now I'm feeling better. (MOVES AROUND)

Now I'm feeling great!! Boy, did I outsmart those dumb dogs. Boy, was I clever. Look at this neat cave. Yep, I'm clever all right. That's me, the clever wolf. Way to go, you lucky guy.

(WALKS TO FEET. GRABS HOLD OF EXTENDED FOOT)

Well, Feet, here we are safe. What did you do, Feet, to help?

FEET: I jumped over the rocks and rivers. I sped across the grassy plains. I swerved and darted and outran those dogs. (FEET RUN IN PLACE)

WOLF: Good Feet! Good Feet!

(WOLF PATS FEET ON HEAD, WALKS TO EARS)

WOLF: (contd) And here are my beautiful, pointed ears. What did you do, Ears, to help?

EARS: I first heard the dogs approaching. I listened to the right and to the left. I knew which way they were coming from. I could tell how close they were coming.

WOLF: Good Ears! Good Ears! (PATS EARS ON HEAD, WALKS TO EYES)
And here are my beautiful eyes. What did you do to help?

EYES: Why, we looked and looked. We pointed the way. We found this very cave where you are safe.

WOLF: Good Eyes! Good Eyes! (PATS EYES ON HEAD) Yep, I'm a pretty smart wolf all right, with lots of good helpers.

(WOLF SPIES TAIL, WALKS TO TAIL)

WOLF: (contd) Ah yes, my tail. What did you do?

(TAIL IS SILENT)

WOLF: (contd) What? You did nothing? You just hung there on the end of me expecting me to carry you along. Bad tail! Bad tail! (WOLF BEGINS HITTING TAIL) Just get out of here. We don't need you. (BEGINS PUSHING TAIL)

EYES, EARS, FEET: No! No! Don't do that!!

WOLF: The tail didn't help. We don't want him. Get out of this cave, Tail!

(ALL PARTS JOIN HANDS, WOLF LAST, TAIL HEADS FOR EXIT, PULLING OTHERS WITH HIM)

EYES, EARS, FEET: Wait. Wait. We are all one body. We need every part. We will all be destroyed with the tail.

DOG: (OFFSTAGE VOICE) Hey, fellow dogs, come help me. I just caught hold of the tail. Come on. We can pull this old wolf out of his hole. Growl! Growl!! Growl!

(ALL ARE PULLED OFF STAGE, MOANING AND GROANING)

— END OF SKIT 5 —

Stories of Jesus

(IN THESE EPISODES, THE VOICE OF JESUS IS AMPLIFIED FROM OFF STAGE. ACTORS STAND CENTER STAGE AS THOUGH ADDRESSING JESUS)

MASTER OF CEREMONIES: We are all different. We are all necessary to God. But how do we learn to overcome old fears, old prejudices? How did Jesus treat persons who were different?

The Bible gives us some examples. Our first example is from Mark 10:46-52, "Jesus Meets Bartemaeus."

SKIT 6: JESUS MEETS BARTEMAEUS
(CAST: BARTIMAEUS, VOICE OF JESUS, NARRATOR)
(SETTING: BLIND BEGGAR, SITTING ON STAGE LEFT, WITH OUTSTRETCHED HANDS, BEGGING)

NARRATOR: They came to Jericho and as Jesus was leaving with his disciples and a large crowd, a blind beggar named Bartimaeus, son of Timaeus, was sitting by the road. When he heard that it was Jesus of Nazareth nearby, he began to shout.

BARTIMAEUS: Jesus! Son of David! Have mercy on me!!

NARRATOR: Jesus stopped and said:

VOICE OF JESUS: Call him!

NARRATOR: So they called the blind man. "Cheer up," they said. "Get up. He is calling you." So he threw off his cloak, jumped up and came to Jesus.

(BARTIMAEUS COMES AND STANDS CENTER STAGE, ARMS RAISED, LOOKING UP)

VOICE OF JESUS: What do you want me to do for you?

BARTIMAEUS: Teacher. I want to see again.

VOICE OF JESUS: Go! Your faith has made you well.

NARRATOR: At once he was able to see and he followed Jesus down the road.

(BARTIMAEUS PANTOMIMES JOY AND EXITS)

NARRATOR: (contd) Jesus looked on him with compassion and healed him.

— END OF SKIT 6 —

MASTER OF CEREMONIES: Another time Jesus encountered a rich, young man. We read his story in Matthew 19:16-22.

SKIT 7: JESUS MEETS RICH, YOUNG RULER
(CAST: YOUNG MAN, VOICE OF JESUS, NARRATOR)
(SETTING: YOUNG MAN IN RICH CLOTHING ENTERS. STANDS CENTER STAGE AND TALKS TO IMAGINARY JESUS)

YOUNG MAN: Teacher. What good thing must I do to receive eternal life?

VOICE OF JESUS: Why do you ask me concerning what is good? There is only one who is good. Keep the commandments if you want to enter life.

YOUNG MAN: What commandments?

VOICE OF JESUS: Do not commit murder, do not commit adultery, do not steal, do not accuse anyone falsely, respect your father and mother and love your neighbor as you love yourself.

YOUNG MAN: I have obeyed all these commandments. What else do I need to do?

VOICE OF JESUS: If you want to be perfect, go and sell all you have and give the money to the poor and you will have riches in heaven, then come and follow me.

NARRATOR: When the young man heard this he went away sad, because he was very rich.

(RICH, YOUNG MAN EXITS)

NARRATOR: Jesus looked on him with compassion and challenged him.

— END OF SKIT 7 —

MASTER OF CEREMONIES: Once Jesus met a Samaritan woman. We read this story in the fourth chapter of John, John 4:5-15.

SKIT 8: JESUS MEETS THE WOMAN OF SAMARIA
(CAST: WOMAN, VOICE OF JESUS, NARRATOR)
(SETTING: IMAGINARY WELL AS MEETING PLACE)

NARRATOR: Jesus and his disciples in Samaria came to a town named Sychar, which was not far from the field that Jacob had given to his son, Joseph. Jacob's well was there and Jesus, tired out by his trip, sat down by the well. It was almost noon. A Samaritan woman came to draw some water and Jesus said to her:

(WOMAN ENTERS)

VOICE OF JESUS: Give me a drink of water.

NARRATOR: His disciples had gone into town to buy food.

WOMAN: You are a Jew and I am a Samaritan so how can you ask me for a drink?

NARRATOR: Jews would not use the same cups and bowls as the Samaritans used.

VOICE OF JESUS: If you only knew what God gives and who it is that is asking you for a drink, you would ask him and he would give you life-saving water.

WOMAN: Sir, you don't have a bucket and the well is deep. Where would you get that life-giving water? It was our ancestor Jacob who gave us this well, he and his sons and his flocks all drank from it. You don't claim to be greater than Jacob, do you?

VOICE OF JESUS: Whoever drinks this water will get thirsty again but whoever drinks the water I give will never be thirsty again. The water that I will give him will become in him a spring which will provide him with life-giving water and give him eternal life.

WOMAN: Sir, give me of that water.

(WOMAN EXITS)

NARRATOR: Jesus looked on her with compassion and offered equality.

— END OF SKIT 8 —

MASTER OF CEREMONIES: Once Jesus met a hated tax collector. We read of this in the fifth chapter of Luke, Luke 5:27.

SKIT 9: JESUS MEETS A TAX COLLECTOR
(CAST: TAX-COLLECTOR, MAN, VOICE OF JESUS, NARRATOR)
(SETTING: TAX COLLECTOR COMES OUT AND SITS. ANOTHER MAN IS STANDING BY)

NARRATOR: After this, Jesus went out and saw a tax collector named Levi sitting in his office. Jesus said to him:

VOICE OF JESUS: Follow me.

NARRATOR: Levi got up, left everything and followed him.

(SEATED MAN GETS UP AND LEAVES. OTHER MAN TURNS CENTER STAGE)

MAN: Why do you eat and drink with tax collectors and other outcasts?

VOICE OF JESUS: People who are well do not need a doctor, but only those who are sick. I have not come to call respectable people to repent, but outcasts.

(ALL CHARACTERS FROM SKITS 6 – 9 COME ONSTAGE: BLIND MAN, RICH YOUNG MAN, SAMARITAN WOMAN AND THE TAX COLLECTOR)

MASTER OF CEREMONIES: Jesus did not avoid people who were different. He never treated them differently or badly. He never acted as if he were better than they were and he told us, "Go and do likewise." (ACTORS EXIT) This concludes our program for today (TONIGHT). Will you all please stand and sing.

HYMN: "Blest Be the Tie that Binds" (THE METHODIST HYMNAL, NO. 306)

Ash Wednesday Observance

INTRODUCTION
Ash Wednesday and the season of Lent are difficult for some children to understand. A meaningful Special Day can be a celebration of this occasion. This can be a weekday afternoon, after-school event followed by a snack supper if you like.

Children ages 5 to 12 will gather in the Fellowship Hall or large classroom. Five additional classrooms will be needed, and set up for the events. A storyteller will be needed in four of these rooms.

PARTICIPANTS
Children
Leader
Four Storytellers

MATERIALS
old sheet
fabric scraps
scissors, glue
sheets
popcorn poppers, popcorn (unpopped)
oyster crackers
paper cups
papier-mache faces (SEE PREPARATION)
string
blindfolds, long pole
paper and pencils

SOURCES FOR MUSIC SUGGESTIONS
"Lonesome Valley" — **The Good Times Songbook**, Abingdon Press, 1974.

PREPARATION

INSTRUCTIONS FOR PAPIER-MACHE, "TEMPTATION" FACES — (TO DO AHEAD OF TIME)

1. Make a round form out of chicken wire, leaving a space large enough to stuff with candy.

2. Straighten out a coat hanger and connect it to the top of the wire form.

3. Tear newspaper into 2 inch wide strips, 15 inches long.

4. Prepare papier-mache (the premixed kind from a hobby or craft shop) according to package directions.

5. Dip the paper strips into the papier-mache and remove any excess.

6. Stuff candy into the hole. (wrapped, hard candy)

7. Drape the wet strips across the wire form in crisscross fashion. Cover the entire form, including the holes.

8. Put on 2 or 3 layers of strips, making sure you cannot see the wire.

9. Allow the form to dry. This could take up to two weeks.

10. When the form is dry, cover the ball with a primer coat of white paint (tempra) to cover up the newsprint.

11. Paint a face on each form. (SEE ILLUSTRATION BELOW FOR EXPRESSIONS TO USE)

12. Hang by coathanger and string.

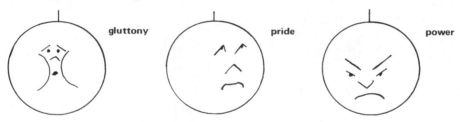

gluttony   pride   power

PROGRAM

LEADER: Today we are starting a new season in the church year, the season of Lent. This season will last 40 days plus the six Sundays of Lent. It is the time of year that leads us up to the celebration of Easter.

This season began because when people thought about how special our celebration of Easter is, they wanted a period of time to get ready for it. The word "Lent" comes from an old Anglo Saxon word that means "Spring" and before these 40 days are over, we will be into the Spring of the year.

In the Bible, the number 40 has always been important. It is used to symbolize a period of cleansing, testing or preparation.

In four of our Church School classrooms, we will be hearing a 40 Days story from the Bible and doing an activity. First we will sing together a song that captures the mood of Lent.

HYMN: "Lonesome Valley" (**THE GOOD TIMES SONGBOOK,** ABINGDON PRESS, 1974)

(CHILDREN GO TO ROOM 1)

Room 1: Noah and the 40 Day Rain

TEACHER: Our first 40 Day's story is one most of you are probably familiar with, the story of Noah and the Ark. This is a very old story, told long before people could write. It is now found in the book of Genesis in our Bible.

The story of Noah takes place at a time when there were many people living on earth, but the story says they were people who did not try to please God at all. They did not love him. They did not thank him for their blessings. They didn't teach their children right from wrong. All in all, it was a sad world with sin everywhere.

This ancient story says God felt sorry he had ever made man and just decided to destroy everything — people, animals and every creature that lived on earth. He would cause a great flood of water to cover the earth.

Then God remembered Noah. Noah really tried to do right and this was especially hard because everyone around him was doing wrong. Noah also taught his sons to do right. God was pleased with Noah and his sons.

And so God told Noah to build a great ship, an ark, and to put his family on board and two of every kind of animal. Noah did as God commanded, even though his neighbors laughed and made fun of him. But then it began to rain. And such a rain! There was a downpour for 40 days and nights, but Noah and his family were safe. The ark floated over the earth for many months until finally it came to rest on a mountain and Noah knew the water was beginning to recede.

At last the day came when they all left the ark and stepped onto dry land. Noah was thankful to God because his life and the lives of his family had been saved, while all other people had perished from the earth.

God then promised that never again would he send another flood to destroy every living creature and that as long as the earth should remain there would be summer and winter, springtime and autumn and day and night. And because God wanted mankind to remember always the promise that he would never again destroy the earth with a flood, he placed in the sky a sign of his promise — a beautiful rainbow. Our sign or symbol for this season of Lent this year is also a rainbow.

(ON FLOOR HAVE AN OLD SHEET WITH 6 ARCS OF A RAINBOW DRAWN ON IT. EACH ARC SHOULD BE LABELED: RED, ORANGE, YELLOW, GREEN, BLUE AND VIOLET. ALSO HAVE LARGE PILES OF FABRIC SCRAPS IN ALL COLORS AND DESIGNS. IN ADDITION, YOU WILL NEED SCISSORS AND GLUE)

INSTRUCTIONS — Have the children cut patches of material in any size and any shape they want. They can then glue these patches to the appropriate arc, with scraps that are predominantly red on the red arc, blue on blue, and so on. Overlap the edges. The patches can be prints, stripes, solids, plaids, etc. When the rainbow is completed, hang the sheet in the Church School hallway for the season of Lent.

(THE CHILDREN GO TO ROOM 2)

Room 2: Moses and the 40 Year Journey

(THE FLOOR TO THIS ROOM IS COVERED WITH SHEETS. POPCORN POPPERS WITHOUT TOPS ARE PLACED AROUND THE ROOM WITH UNPOPPED POPCORN IN THEM. WHEN THE CHILDREN ARE SEATED ON THE FLOOR, NOT TOO CLOSE TO THE POPPERS, THE POPPERS ARE PLUGGED IN. THE STORYTELLER TRIES TO PACE THE STORY SO THAT THE POPCORN WILL BEGIN POPPING AT THE CORRECT TIME)

TEACHER: Our next 40's story is about Moses and the great task he had of leading all the children of Israel out of the land of Egypt into the promised land. You know the story of how Moses pleaded with the great Pharoah of Egypt to let his people go and how he had to send plagues on the land. Remember how he had to lead them across the Red Sea and into the wilderness?

God, through Moses, did many wonderful signs, but once the people had escaped and had arrived in the desert, they began to complain and worry. They had arrived in a place called the Wilderness of Sin. Like fretful children, the Israelites began to find fault with Moses. First one thing and then another displeased them. They could find so little food to eat in the great wilderness that they began to grow hungry. Then they forgot how much they had suffered in Egypt — how they were slaves there and badly treated. They forgot how many times God had helped them out of trouble. They thought only of their hunger and unhappiness.

They said, "We wish we had never left Egypt, for there at least we had plenty to eat. We had rather have died there than in this dreary old country."

The people complained to Moses and it made him very sad. But God said, "I did not bring you this far to let you starve. I will provide food for you."

The next morning, the ground was covered with small white objects. "What is it?" the people asked. In their language, the words, "what is this?" are "man hu" and so the food afterwards came to be called "manna."

Moses told the people that God had sent this food to them. "Go and gather it," he said.

(AS THE POPCORN POPPERS HEAT UP WITHOUT TOPS, THE POPPING CORN WILL FLY ALL OVER THE ROOM LIKE MANNA FROM HEAVEN. LET THE CHILDREN GATHER IT OFF THE SHEETS AND EAT IT)

(IN AN ADJOINING ROOM, THE TEACHER HAS PLACED OYSTER-CRACKERS IN SHALLOW CONTAINERS ALL OVER THE ROOM — ON FURNITURE, ON CHAIRS, PIANOS, ETC.)

TEACHER: (contd) Now children, there is one thing about manna. God told the children of Israel only to gather enough for one day. It would not last over night.

(GIVE EACH CHILD A SMALL PAPER CUP)

Go into the next room and find more manna. But only get enough for your one cup.

(CHILDREN ENGAGE IN THIS ACTIVITY, THEN RETURN TO ROOM 2)

The Israelites lived for 40 years in the wilderness, and God sent manna to them every morning, until they came to the land of Canaan.

(THE CHILDREN GO TO ROOM 3)

Room 3: Jesus and 40 Days in the Wilderness

TEACHER: The 40 Days story we associate most closely with Lent is the 40 days that Jesus spent in the wilderness before he began his ministry.

After Jesus' baptism in the River Jordan, when God's voice spoke from heaven saying, "This is my beloved Son," Jesus went off alone into the wilderness for 40 days, to think about his life and to prepare for his ministry. While he was there he was faced with three great temptations.

Jesus was faint and hungry and he felt the temptation to turn the stones into loaves of bread. But then he said, "No! Man shall not live by bread alone but by every word of God." Although he was hungry and faint, Jesus would not use his great power to please himself.

In the next temptation Jesus felt, he was on the topmost part of the temple of Jerusalem. And the temptation came: "If you expect people to believe that you are really God's son, you must show some great sign. Now cast yourself down to the ground and trust God to protect you and keep your bones from being broken." But Jesus knew that the Scriptures had forbidden anyone to tempt God in such a foolish manner.

In the third temptation, Jesus imagined himself on a high hill where he could see all the kingdoms of the world: "These can all be yours if you will turn from worshipping God." But again Jesus stood strong, remembering the Scriptures. "The Lord God is the only Being who should be worshipped."

Jesus was tempted in every way that people on earth are tempted. Still he did no wrong. We want to now destroy the temptations Jesus faced.

From the ceiling are hanging three large papier-mache faces: Gluttony, Pride and Power. (SEE INSTRUCTIONS FOR MAKING THESE FACES IN THE PREPARATION SECTION)

(CHILDREN, BLINDFOLDED, WILL TAKE TURNS HITTING AT THE FACES WITH A LONG POLE, TRYING TO BREAK THEM)

(THE CHILDREN GO TO ROOM 4)

Room 4: Moses and 40 Days on the Mountain

TEACHER: Our final 40 Days story is again about Moses. After the Israelites were in the wilderness, safe from the Egyptians and being fed by God, Moses wanted to talk to God and understand what he was supposed to do.

So Moses went up on Mt. Sanai, a large, smoking mountain. He told the people to be obedient until he returned. For 40 days Moses listened to God's words and the Lord gave him two flat tablets of stone upon which he had written the Ten Commandments.

For our last activity, we want to sit quietly and listen to God speaking to us and then write down on the paper in front of you something you will do these 40 days before Easter to bring you closer to God. Write a covenant for yourself. How will you spend your forty days?

SPRING
MARCH/APRIL/MAY

SPECIAL DAYS IN SPRING

The great Jubilee occasion of Easter should be the highlight, the peak celebration of your Church School year. Observe this occasion with a celebration for the entire Church School on Easter morning that culminates a study of change.

Confirmation may also be a part of your Easter festival. Let your confirmands dramatize their new relationship to the church by "Dedicating a Stone."

In addition, during this season of newness, fresh beginnings and gentle weather, you can enjoy spring cleaning of the Church School, honor Mothers with a special open house featuring drama and art, and have a parade that proclaims the joy of our Christian heritage.

Easter Morning Celebration — Peter Before and After *

INTRODUCTION

This is an Easter morning Sunday School celebration for combined children's classes and their parents. The suggested setting is the Fellowship Hall.

PARTICIPANTS

Leader
Pre-schoolers
Grades 1 and 2
Grades 3 and 4
Grades 5 and 6
Congregation

MATERIALS

projects as indicated in script (SEE INSTRUCTIONS IN PREPARATION SECTION)
posterboard with words

SOURCES FOR MUSIC SUGGESTIONS

"He's Alive" — by Avery and Marsh, copyright 1970, Hope Publishing Co.
"All Things Bright and Beautiful" — the Methodist Hymnal, No. 34.
"Christ the Lord is Risen Today" — the Methodist Hymnal, No. 439.

*Reprinted version of **Peter, Before and After**, by Judy Gattis Smith, copyright 1981, Arthur Meriwether, Inc. Used by permission.

INSTRUCTIONS FOR EGG MEN PLANTS

Begin two weeks ahead of time.

STEP 1: Prepare eggshells for each child, leaving an opening at the top.

STEP 2: Fill eggshells with dirt.

STEP 3: Draw face on eggshell, using paint or soft markers.

STEP 4: Plant (with the children) grass seeds in the dirt.

STEP 5: Leave eggs in sunny place. Water as needed. Grass seeds grow as hair.

One five-year-old called this an eggplant.

INSTRUCTIONS FOR FABRIC FLOWERS

STEP 1: Gather fabric scraps in different colors, prints and textures.

STEP 2: Draw petal patterns on paper and cut out.

STEP 3: Pin paper patterns to fabric and cut out.

STEP 4: Use green pipecleaners. Glue a pipecleaner to each petal around the edge of the petal and hanging down as stem.

STEP 5: Put several petals together around flower center (may be bought at Craft store) holding stems.

STEP 6: Wrap one end of a long pipe cleaner tightly around stems.

STEP 7: Leaves may also be added.

INSTRUCTIONS FOR 3—D TREES

STEP 1: Cut a tree shape out of poster paper.

STEP 2: Choose colors for branches and leaves (light green or white for apple blossoms, etc.) Cut small squares of tissue paper (about 3") in the chosen colors.

STEP 3: Spread a thin coat of glue on tree (small section at a time).

STEP 4: Prepare the tissue squares by folding one square of tissue paper around the end of a pencil. Set it down on the glued area, using the pencil end to push the tissue into the glued area.

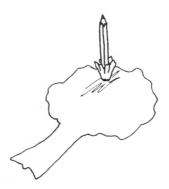

STEP 5: Glue tissue fluffs very close together to make the tree look fluffy and spring-like.

INSTRUCTIONS FOR CELLOPHANE BUTTERFLIES

STEP 1: Draw and cut butterfly shape from black construction paper. Use folded paper so that you end up with two sides of butterfly exactly the same.

STEP 2: Cut holes in any design you wish.

STEP 3: Make another identical shape.

STEP 4: Cut piece of cellophane (colored) paper large enough to cover the holes.

STEP 5: Staple or glue the three pieces together: one butterfly shape, one piece colored cellophane, identical butterfly shape on top. Cellophane will show through holes.

STEP 6: Hang by a string.

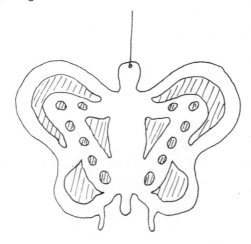

ORDER OF SERVICE
Call to Worship
Song: "He's Alive"
Scripture
Responsive Sentences
Easter Show and Tell: Things that Change
Hymn: "All Things Bright and Beautiful"
Peter Before and After
Song: "He's Alive"
Action Response
Closing Scripture
Hymn: "Christ the Lord is Risen Today"

LITURGY
LEADER: On this Easter morning we proclaim the Good News — Jesus lives!

SONG: "He's Alive" (AVERY AND MARSH, HOPE PUBLISHING CO.) (THIS IS A HAND CLAPPING, FINGER SNAPPING, WHISTLING, SHOUTING SONG OF RESURRECTION)

SCRIPTURE: You, Lord, in the beginning created the earth and with your own hands you made the Heavens. They will disappear, but you will remain. They will all wear out like clothes. You will fold them up like a coat, and they will be changed like clothes. But you are always the same and your life never ends. (Hebrews 1:10-12)

LEADER: Our bodies change. We grow.

CONGREGATION: (RESPONSE) Everything changes but God.

LEADER: Winter turns into Spring.

CONGREGATION: Everything changes but God.

LEADER: We learn more. Our minds expand.

CONGREGATION: Everything changes but God.

LEADER: Seeds in the earth become flowers.

CONGREGATION: Everything changes but God.

LEADER: We will all die but live again.

CONGREGATION: Everything changes but God.

LEADER: Change is the theme of our Easter program today and the children of our Church School have a Show and Tell time for us now on "Things that Change."

Things that Change
PRE-SCHOOLERS: Seeds change into Plants.

(CHILDREN COME FORWARD AND SHOW THEIR EGG-MEN PLANTS AND MAY EXPLAIN ABOUT THEM IF THEY WISH)

GRADES 1 AND 2: Bare trees turn to leafy branches.

(CHILDREN COME FORWARD AND SHOW THEIR "3-D" TREES AND MAY EXPLAIN ABOUT THEM IF THEY WISH)

GRADES 3 AND 4: Bulbs turn into flowers.

(CHILDREN COME FORWARD AND SHOW THEIR FABRIC FLOWERS AND MAY EXPLAIN ABOUT THEM IF THEY WISH)

GRADES 5 AND 6: Caterpillars turn into butterflies.

(CHILDREN COME FORWARD AND SHOW THEIR CELLOPHANE BUTTERFLIES AND MAY EXPLAIN ABOUT THEM IF THEY WISH)

HYMN: "All Things Bright and Beautiful" (THE METHODIST HYMNAL, NO. 34)

Peter Before and After

LEADER: One of the most exciting things in the world is to see people grow and change from weak to strong, from clumsy to skillful, from ignorant to wise, from scared to brave. We wee an example of amazing growth in the life of one of the disciples — Peter. It is an Easter story and a story for all times.

Peter was a big, strong man, muscular from lifting heavy nets of fish and steering his fishing boats through storms and tempests. He was tanned from his life in the sun. Jesus chose him first to be his disciple. Peter was the first to proclaim that Jesus was the Messiah. He was an eager, enthusiastic disciple. And yet, Peter was a weak man. Let's look at this story as it appears in our Bible and try to experience what Peter experienced.

Jesus had gathered all of the disciples together in an Upper Room for the celebration of Passover — their last supper together. That supper had been a strange time. Jesus had shared bread and wine with his followers and asked them to remember him whenever they gathered in this way. He had washed their feet like a servant. Jesus then revealed to them his coming betrayal and death. He even predicted that none of his disciples would be willing to stand by him when he got in trouble.

Peter reacted with astonishment. He couldn't understand what Jesus was saying. He jumped to his feet in his excitement.

Remember a time in your own life when you were puzzled, confused. Peter asked Jesus, "Where are you going, Lord?"

Let's stand and practice this sentence a few times, putting the accent on different syllables.

(CONGREGATION STANDS)

Where are you going, Lord?
Where are **you** going, Lord?
Where are you **going**, Lord?

Feel yourself getting more and more agitated and anxious. Now let's use these three sentences in the context of Scripture. We will read John 13:36-38. The Congregation begins by accenting "where."

LEADER: (contd) Three times we will ask this question of Jesus:

CONGREGATION: **Where** are you going, Lord?

LEADER: Jesus answered, "You cannot follow me now where I am going."

CONGREGATION: Where are **you** going, Lord?

LEADER: Jesus answered, "You cannot follow me now where I am going."

CONGREGATION: Where are you **going,** Lord?

LEADER: Jesus answered, "You cannot follow me now where I am going, but later you will follow me." Peter replied, "I am ready to die for you." Again, let's affirm Peter's statement three times, with the accent on different words. First, we will accent the "I;" second, "ready;" and third, "die." (PRACTICE WITH CONGREGATION) I am ready to die for you. I am **ready** to die for you. I am ready to **die** for you. Feel the conviction, the assurance Peter felt. Now, let us read it in the context of Scripture.

CONGREGATION: I am ready to die for you.

LEADER: Jesus answered, "Are you really ready to die for me?"

CONGREGATION: I am **ready** to die for you.

LEADER: Jesus answered, "Are you really ready to die for me?"

CONGREGATION: I am ready to **die** for you.

LEADER: Jesus answered, "Are you really ready to die for me? I tell you the truth. Before the rooster crows, you will say three times that you do not know me." And Jesus' prediction was true as we read in the Bible. Let's try to experience what this must have been like. Suppose you had done something wrong and someone found out and accused you of it. But you deny it. Say the words, "I didn't do it," and accent different words. First, we will accent the "I;" second, "didn't;" and third, "do." (PRACTICE WITH CONGREGATION) I didn't do it. I **didn't** do it. I didn't **do** it.

Let yourself get more and more agitated. We will pretend we are Peter and are saying the words, "I don't know him" three times. Begin by accenting the "I;" second, "don't;" and third, "him." (PRACTICE WITH CONGREGATION) I don't know him. I **don't** know him. I don't know **him.** Each time become more emphatic. Become agitated. Use your arms, hands and fists. (PRACTICE A FEW TIMES)

Now let's read Luke 22:54-62. They arrested Jesus and took him away into the house of the high priest and Peter followed far behind. A fire had been lit in the center of the courtyard and Peter joined those who were sitting around it. When one of the servant girls saw him sitting there at the fire, she looked straight at him and said, "This man, too, was with him!"

But Peter denied it.

CONGREGATION: I don't know him.

LEADER: After a little while a man noticed him and said, "You are one of them, too. But Peter answered:

CONGREGATION: I **don't** know him.

71

LEADER: And about an hour later another man insisted strongly, "There isn't any doubt that this man was with him because he also is a Galilean!" But Peter answered,

CONGREGATION: I don't know **him**.

LEADER: At once, while he was still speaking, a rooster crowed. The Lord turned around and looked straight at Peter and Peter remembered the Lord's words, how he had said, "Before the rooster crows today, you will say three times that you do not know me." Peter went out and wept bitterly. Peter's mind and heart felt as if they would break; would explode with the agony of his failure. He had been so sure, so self righteous. Tears of despair flooded his eyes. His body shook with sobs. He stumbled out of the shadowy courtyard as dawn appeared and Friday morning, the day of Jesus' crucifixion, began. (CONGREGATION IS SEATED)

This was Peter; a coward, deserting his friend, his teacher and his Master in his time of greatest need. Peter: weak, terribly frightened and ashamed of his own behavior. But the Bible story does not end here. We read about Peter again. The Crucifixion of Jesus took place, but also the Resurrection. And Peter was the disciple who ran to find the empty tomb — who picked up the empty burial clothes — who heard the angel proclaim, "He is not here. He is risen."

And now it is several weeks after the resurrection of Jesus. The setting is outside the Temple of Jerusalem. There at the "Beautiful Gate," as it was called, was a man who had been lame all his life. Imagine yourself as that man. As you sit in your chair, try to imagine your feet numb with no feeling at all. Try to imagine your legs withered and useless. Close your eyes and concentrate on feeling the helplessness of a cripple.

At three o'clock in the afternoon, the hour for prayers, Peter came to the temple. You are going to reach out and beg money from this man. Stretch out your hand — slowly, stiffly. It is painful even to move your arms though there is at least feeling there. (PAUSE) Open your fingers. (PAUSE) Reach up. You say nothing but beg with your face. (PAUSE)

Peter looked at him and said, "I have no money at all but I will give you what I have; in the name of Jesus Christ of Nazareth, I order you to walk."

With your outstretched hand, feel Peter taking your hand. Close your fingers around his. Feel the strength that comes into your body. (PAUSE) Concentrate on your toes. Wiggle them. Feel them coming to life. Feel your ankles. Feel life pulsing through them. Slowly — slowly, begin to stand up. Feel your legs, wobbly at first, getting stronger and stronger. Stand up. Stomp your feet. Move them quickly. Jump up and down. Begin to move about. The Bible says, "Then he went into the Temple with Peter, walking and jumping and praising God."

Sing now as if you were the lame man. Walk around, jump around and sing.

SONG: "He's Alive" (AVERY AND MARSH, HOPE PUBLISHING CO.) (STANDING) (CONGREGATION IS SEATED)

LEADER: It was Peter who performed this great miracle — a man lame from birth could walk. Naturally a large crowd of people gathered around and Peter began to tell them about Jesus. Throughout the book of Acts, we read about Peter's great and powerful preaching. At one time

LEADER: (contd) he converted three thousand people at a single preaching. He preached with boldness, completely devoid of any fear. This was Peter, the coward, the failure. Something tremendous happened in his life and turned his whole life around. He was arrested for his preaching, but when he was brought before the High Council and strongly commanded to preach no more, he answered, "We cannot but speak of the things which we have seen and heard." Peter, who had been afraid to admit before a simple serving girl that he even knew Jesus, stood boldly before rulers and judges proclaiming the Lordship of Jesus to all. What do you think made the difference in Peter? The facts of Easter morning caused the change in Peter. In the Bible, then, we have seen two pictures of Peter — Peter before, and Peter after. Think about how you feel about Peter. Many times we express our feelings by things we do. For example, here are ten things we want to do. Everyone join in. (THE FOLLOWING WORDS ARE WRITTEN ON POSTERBOARD)

(LIST THE FOLLOWING EMOTIONAL REACTIONS: BOO, CLAP, CHEER, STOMP YOUR FEET, WAVE, MAKE A FIST AND SHAKE IT, HIDE YOUR FACE WITH YOUR HANDS, POINT ACCUSINGLY AT SOMEONE, PAT YOUR NEIGHBOR ON THE BACK, MAKE A BIG KISS ON THE BACK OF YOUR HAND AND THROW IT)

LEADER: (contd) Now think carefully back over the stories of Peter. Which one of these ten responses would you like to make to Peter when he was afraid and denied knowing Jesus?

(AUDIENCE CHOOSES AND TELLS WHY THEY MAKE THE CHOICE, THEN MAKES RESPONSE)

LEADER: (contd) Now, which one of these responses would you make to Peter when he was brave and courageous and healing the sick?

(AGAIN AUDIENCE CHOOSES, TELLS WHY AND MAKES RESPONSE)

LEADER: (contd) Think about this: How could Peter change so much? What made the difference? Have you ever known anyone who changed from being scared to brave? Have you? Hear these final words about change.

"Listen to this secret truth, we shall not all die, but when the last trumpet sounds, we shall all be changed in an instant, as quickly as the blinking of an eye. For when the trumpet sounds, the dead will be raised never to die again and we shall all be changed." (1 Corinthians 15:51)

HYMN: "Christ the Lord Is Risen Today" (THE METHODIST HYMNAL, NO. 439)

Confirmation Liturgy

INTRODUCTION

One of the highlights and special days in the life of any church is when young people decide to join the church and become full members. In many churches, this follows weeks and months of study in which students learn about God, Jesus, the Bible, their particular denomination and make a decision to publicly confirm their faith. Most churches have their own rituals and rites for this very sacred and special occasion. But, following this, many classes want a way to personalize and dramatize their celebration of confirmation. If your church has a church garden or an outdoor spot where a large, decorative rock can become a part of the landscape, consider this service of celebration. The entire congregation joins in the service, either processing from the sanctuary to the outside, or with a few changes, the service may be used within the sanctuary.

PARTICIPANTS

Leader
New Members, Congregation
Trumpet Player

MATERIALS

trumpet
large, decorative rock or stone
slips of paper with Bible verses
tape

SOURCES FOR MUSIC SUGGESTIONS

"God of Our Fathers" — found in most hymnals
"They'll Know We are Christians by Our Love" — **Genesis Songbook**, Agape Press, 1973.
"Rock of Ages" — the Methodist Hymnal, No. 120.

LITURGY

(CONGREGATION, LED BY THE NEWLY CONFIRMED MEMBERS OF THE CHURCH, GATHER AT AN OUTDOOR SPOT. THEY ARE LED TO THIS SPOT BY A TRUMPET, PLAYING, "GOD OF OUR FATHERS." WHEN ALL HAVE ASSEMBLED, LEADER BEGINS)

LEADER: Why are we here, in God's out-of-doors beside His church?

NEW MEMBERS: To celebrate the fact that we are now full members of this church. To hear our story. To declare in visible form our dedication.

HYMN: "They'll Know We Are Christians by Our Love" (**GENESIS SONGBOOK**, AGAPE PRESS, 1973)

LEADER: What is the story that you would hear?

NEW MEMBERS: The story of our ancestor in the faith, Joshua, the man who was chosen to follow Moses.

LEADER: Hear then the Scriptures, Joshua 1:1-9.

(TRUMPET FANFARE BEFORE EACH READING FROM JOSHUA)

LEADER: (contd) After the death of the Lord's servant Moses, the Lord spoke to Moses' helper, Joshua, son of Nun. He said, "My servant Moses is dead. Get ready now, you and all the people of Israel, and cross the Jordan River into the land that I am giving them. As I told Moses, I have given you and all my people the entire land that you will be marching over. Your borders will reach from the desert in the south to the Lebanon Mountains in the north; from the great Euphrates River in the east through the Hittite country, to the Mediterranean Sea in the west. Joshua, no one will be able to defeat you as long as you live. I will be with you as I was with Moses. I will always be with you; I will never abandon you. Be determined and confident, for you will be the leader of these people as they occupy this land which I promised their ancestors. Just be determined, be confident; and make sure that you obey the whole Law that my servant Moses gave you. Do not neglect any part of it and you will succeed wherever you go. Be sure that the Book of the Law is always read in your worship. Study it day and night and make sure that you obey everything written in it. Then you will be prosperous and successful. Remember that I have commanded you to be determined and confident! Do not be afraid or discouraged, for I, the Lord your God, am with you wherever you go."

NEW MEMBERS: Joshua's story is our own.

LEADER: But after Joshua heard God's word, he called the people together and spoke to them thus: Joshua 24:14. (King James Version)

(TRUMPET FANFARE)

"Now therefore, fear the Lord and serve him in sincerity and in truth . . . and if it seems evil unto you to serve the Lord, choose you this day whom ye will serve . . . but as for me and my house we will serve the Lord."

And the people answered and said, "God forbid that we should forsake the Lord to serve other gods."

NEW MEMBERS: Joshua's story is our own. We choose this day to serve the Lord.

LEADER: Hear Joshua 24:22-24. (King James Version)

(TRUMPET FANFARE)

LEADER: (contd) And Joshua said unto the people, "Ye are witnesses against yourself that ye have chosen you the Lord, to serve him." And they said, "We are witnesses." And the people said unto Joshua, "The Lord our God will we serve and his voice will we obey."

NEW MEMBERS: Joshua's story is our own.

LEADER: Now hear Joshua 24:25-27.

(TRUMPET FANFARE)

LEADER: (contd) So Joshua made a convenant for the people that day, and there at Shechem he gave them laws and rules to follow. Joshua wrote these commands in the book of the Law of God. Then he took a large stone and set it up under the oak tree in the Lord's sanctuary. He said to all the people, "This stone will be our witness. It has heard all the words that the Lord has spoken to us. So it will be a witness against you, to keep you from rebelling against your God."

NEW MEMBERS: Joshua's story is our own and we too would place a stone to be our witness.

(BRING FORWARD DECORATIVE STONE AND PLACE PARTLY IN THE GROUND)

LEADER: Stones are permanent, visible, enduring. A visible reminder, to all who have come to celebrate with you here, of who you have chosen to serve. In the unfolding days and the unfolding years you will pass this stone and you will remember, as the followers of Joshua remembered, the meaning of their stone. And perhaps one day your children may say, "What does that stone mean? Why is it here?" and you will say, "That stone is a reminder of the day I chose to follow God."

(EACH NEW MEMBER READS FROM A SMALL SLIP OF PAPER A BIBLE VERSE ABOUT A ROCK AND THEN TAPES THE VERSE ON THE ROCK)

NEW MEMBERS: The Lord is my rock and my fortress and my deliverer; my God, my strength, in whom I will trust. (Psalms 18:2 King James Version)

Who is a rock save our God? (Psalms 18:31 King James Version)

Thou art my rock and my fortress. (Psalms 31:3 King James Version)

Set my feet upon a rock. (Psalms 40:2 Revised Standard Version)

I will say unto God, my rock, why hast thou forgotten me? (Psalms 42:9 King James Version)

Thou art my rock and my fortress. (Psalms 71:3 King James Version)

Think of the rock from which you came, the quarry from which you were cut. (Isaiah 51:1)

They drank from the spiritual rock that went with them, and that rock was Christ himself. (1 Cor. 10:4)

God is the rock. His work is perfect. (Deuteronomy 32:4 King James Version)

(CONSULT A CONCORDANCE TO THE BIBLE IF YOU NEED OTHER VERSES ABOUT ROCKS — KING JAMES VERSION)

HYMN: "Rock of Ages" (THE METHODIST HYMNAL, NO. 120)

LEADER: (BENEDICTION) Be strong and of a good courage, be not afraid, neither be thou dismayed, for the Lord thy God is with thee withersoever thou goest. (Joshua 1:9 King James Version)

Spring Cleaning Day

INTRODUCTION

No matter how good your janitorial service, no matter how neat a teacher or class may be, the time comes when old Church School material piles up, outdated pictures do not find their way back to the files and a look of clutter fills your classroom.

A Spring cleaning day can be a Special Day in the Church School. Choose a balmy Saturday, invite all the Church School children (Grades 1 to 6) and teachers, wear old clothes and set to work.

PARTICIPANTS

Leader
Storyteller
Four Leaders, 1 for each team
Students for teams

MATERIALS

old clothes
colored cards
refreshments
cleaning supplies as necessary

SOURCES FOR MUSIC SUGGESTIONS

"If You're Saved and You Know It" — **Salvation Songs for Children**, Book 4. Child Evangelism Fellowship, Warrenton, MO, 63383.

"Joy, Joy, Joy, Joy Down in My Heart" — **Salvation Songs for Children**, Book 3. (see above)

ACTIVITY

(GATHER IN THE FELLOWSHIP HALL OR A LARGE CLASSROOM. AS THE CHILDREN ARRIVE, GIVE EACH ONE A CARD WITH A COLOR ON IT)

WAKE UP AND SING TIME: (SUGGESTED SONGS)

"If You're Happy and You Know It" (**SALVATION SONGS FOR CHILDREN**, BOOK 4, CHILD EVANGELISM FELLOWSHIP)

"Joy, Joy, Joy, Joy Down in my Heart" (**SALVATION SONGS FOR CHILDREN**, BOOK 3, CHILD EVANGELISM FELLOWSHIP)

LEADER: Before we begin our work, boys and girls, we have a story for you. This is a folktale that comes from the land of Wales.

Old Man in the Cottage

STORYTELLER: Once upon a time in a far away land there lived a good, kind, old farmer and his wife. They lived happily in a little white, tiny white, neat white, clean white cottage.

Every night the little old woman washed the dishes and the little old man dried the dishes. Then the little old woman swept the floor and the little old man emptied the dishwater.

Now this was long ago before the time of dishwashers and garbage disposals and in the dishwater were all the scraps from the day — tea leaves and potato peelings, apple cores and onion skins, and egg shells and very dirty water.

And every night, just about the same time, the little old man would walk out the back door, carrying the dishwater and dump it over a little low wall beside his house.

Day after day, year after year, the little old woman and the little old man did the very same thing, in the very same way.

But one night, just as the dishwater had gone sloshing over the wall, the little old man heard a voice.

"Oh dear me! Oh dear me! I wish you wouldn't do that."

The old man looked to the right. He looked to the left — but he saw no one.

Still he heard the voice. "Oh dear! Oh dear! I wish you wouldn't do that."

"But I always do it," he replied. Still he saw no one.

Then he looked over the low wall where he always swished the dishwater and he saw something he had never seen before — a crack in the earth. And as he peered into the crack he saw a tiny little street just like his own street and a tiny little white cottage just like his own cottage. And there was a funny, little man, very, very small.

But what a dreadful state the street and house were in. There were potato peelings on the chimney, tea leaves splashed on the windows, onion skins and apple peel all over the roof and greasy, dirty water dripping down the wall. And the tiny little man was weeping.

"Sometimes," he sobbed, "the water goes down the chimney and puts out the fire."

"And sometimes," he sobbed even louder, "my wife has clean clothes hanging on the line."

Well, the old farmer was very upset. Of course, he did not want to cause all this trouble for the tiny, tiny man. But what was he to do? He had always sloshed the dishwater over the little wall right after supper.

He thought and he worried and he asked his wife about it, but they could think of no answer and he continued to throw the dishwater over the low wall every evening right after supper.

Finally, the old farmer had an idea. He would make a different door on the other side of the house! He got excited and called in the builders. They bricked up the old door and made a new one on the other side.

Now the old farmer could still take out his dirty dishwater every evening right after supper. But now it didn't land on the tiny, tiny family in the tiny, tiny cottage.

It was a lot of trouble and cost a lot of money, but the old farmer and his wife never regretted it, especially on Saturday nights when the happy tiny, tiny family would come for a visit.

LEADER: Well, that was a pretty drastic action for pretty drastic reasons, but we too have litter and clutter that we need to get rid of this morning. As you came in this morning you were given a card with a special color on it. This is the team you will be working with. We have four cleaning teams. Please gather together into your groups now.

(ADULT LEADER OR TEACHER FOR EACH TEAM STANDS. THE CHILDREN IN EACH COLOR GROUP GATHER AROUND THE LEADER OF THEIR TEAM)

LEADER: (contd) When each team has finished its work, the children can come back here for refreshments.

Clean Up

Arrange these suggested cleaning tasks to suit your own cleaning needs.

RED TEAM — Collects old literature and stacks it for recycling. Also files story pictures and posters in the appropriate place.

BLUE TEAM — Organizes supplies. Cleans out cabinets in Church School rooms, putting in new supplies where needed. Suggested for each room: scissors, felt-tipped pens, glue, pencils, crayons, masking tape, paper. Other supplies should be kept in a central supply closet.

GREEN TEAM — Basic cleaning of windows, woodwork, furniture. May divide this team up into different groups for each room.

YELLOW TEAM:— Picks up litter, bottles and debris around the church, inside and out.

Heritage Sunday — Parade of Old Testament Heroes

INTRODUCTION

In the church and Church School we are called to remember our heritage: who we are as a people, where we came from, who our ancestors are in the faith. An appropriate Special Day is a day to celebrate Old Testament heroes. A good way to capture the feeling this day generates is with a parade. This parade may be used as the opening part of a church worship service or it may stand alone as simply a parade. The sanctuary, with the long aisles in many of our churches, the pews for watchers, (for there must be watchers as well as marchers at a parade), the organ and other instruments, all make a perfect setting for a church parade.

PARTICIPANTS

Church School Classes
Music Director
Musicians
Leader
Congregation

MATERIALS

costumes and props as indicated (SEE COSTUMES AND PROPS)
musical instruments
refreshments

SOURCES FOR MUSIC SUGGESTIONS

"Marching with the Heroes" — **Singing Worship**, Edith Lowell Thomas, Abingdon Press.

"Who Built the Ark?" — **Children's Liturgies**, Virginia Sloyan and Gabe Huck, editors, Liturgical Conference, Inc., 1330 Massachusetts Ave., N.W., Washington, D.C. 20015, 1970.

"I Sing a Song of the Saints of God" — **Rejoice and Sing Praise**, compiled by Evelyn Andre and Jeneil Menefee, Abingdon Press, 1977.

"Go Down Moses" — **Good Times Songbook**, James Leisy, Abingdon Press, 1974.

"Women of Israel Dance" — **Signs, Songs and Stories**, Virginia Sloyan, editor, Liturgical Conference, Inc., 1330 Massachusetts Ave., N.W., Washington, D.C. 20015, 1974.

"Only a Boy Named David" — **Sing and Be Happy Songs for Children**, Rodeheaver Co., Winona Lake, Indiana 46591.

"Shalom" — **Genesis Songbook**, Agape Press, 1973.

COSTUMES AND PROPS

Musical instruments for brass band made up of church School students

Nursery procession — 3 and 4 year olds with animal masks or costumes for a Noah's Ark procession

Kindergarten procession — 5 year olds, some with sheep headdresses, some with crowns, some with shepherd crooks for David procession

First and Second Grade procession — 6 and 7 year olds in robes and headdresses for Moses procession

Third and Fourth Grade procession — 8 and 9 year olds, some in multicolored robes, some dressed as Egyptians with elaborate eye makeup for Joseph procession

Fifth and Sixth Grade procession — 10 and 11 year olds dressed in robes and headdresses for the Time of Judges parade. They will need tambourines and finger cymbals.

Make the costumes as colorful and creative as possible. The pomp and spectacle shows our reverence for what we celebrate. There is no such thing as a bashful parade, and while your procession should strive for dignity and reverence, there should also be a festive air of celebration, as characterizes all parades.

PREPARATION

Probably the easiest way to organize your parade is to have each Church School class responsible for arranging their own costumes (maybe making them) and practicing separately their procession and performance. On the day of the parade all classes can come together, thus preserving the spontaneity and festive air.

Each class will want to study their special hero in more detail before the parade. A music director can work with each class and the band in their musical numbers, and/or coordinate the activities.

PRESENTATION

LEADER: The Bible gives us the following admonition: "Think of the past, of the time long ago. Ask your fathers to tell you what happened. Ask the old men to tell of the past." (Deuteronomy 32:7) Remember the stories of your ancestors in the faith.

This is the reason for our coming together today — to remember and celebrate our ancestors in the faith, to recall the Bible stories of Old Testament heroes. We want to walk in the footsteps of these heroes — seeing what they saw, feeling what they felt. Let the parade of heroes begin!

PROCESSION OF BRASS BAND — (BEGIN WITH BRASS BAND AND ORGAN PLAYING "MARCHING WITH THE HEROES" FROM **SINGING WORSHIP**, ABINGDON PRESS. THE CONGREGATION MAY SING ALONG. BAND MARCHES TO FRONT OF CHURCH AND IS SEATED)

LEADER: Our first ancestors in the faith were nomads moving from place to place on the edges of the desert. They were always searching for lifegiving springs of water where there would be grass enough for their precious sheep and goats. An Oasis in the desert. After supper at the Oasis,

LEADER: (contd) the families would gather around a campfire and hear and tell wonderful stories. Everyone would listen as the oldest member of the family would tell and retell a treasured story. The very earliest stories had a growing awareness of a single, important God. He was the creator and ruler of the world. He had a Holy Will which men were to obey.

One of these first stories told of a great flood that covered the earth. But one good man, Noah, and his family, survived the flood and saved a pair of all the animals and promised to remain true to God.

PROCESSION OF NURSERY CHILDREN: (AS ANIMALS IN THE ARK. THEY MAY WEAR PAPER BAG MASKS OR ANIMAL COSTUMES. THEY MARCH IN TO ORGAN MUSIC OR MUSIC BY THE BAND. THEY ASSEMBLE AT THE FRONT OF THE CHURCH AND SING. SUGGESTED SONG— "WHO BUILT THE ARK?" **CHILDREN'S LITURGIES**, LITURGICAL CONFERENCE, INC.)

(FOLLOWING THE SINGING, THEY ARE SEATED AT THE FRONT OF THE CHURCH)

LEADER: (contd) Later the stories heard around the campfires were about more recent, if dimly remembered, heroes. One was a hero named Joseph. He had trials and adventures. He was sold into slavery by his brothers. He was an interpreter of dreams. Later he became a wise ruler in Egypt. And when a great famine hit the land, he saved Egypt as well as his own people from starvation by using his skills and talents. In all the stories about Joseph, he always remained true to his God.

PROCESSION OF THIRD AND FOURTH GRADERS: (ENTER TO MUSIC. THEY ARE DRESSED IN ISRAELITE COSTUMES OF ROBES AND HEADDRESSES, OR EGYPTIAN COSTUMES. SOME CARRY LARGE EGYPTIAN FANS. THEY ASSEMBLE AT THE FRONT OF THE CHURCH AND SING. SUGGESTED SONG — "I SING A SONG OF THE SAINTS OF GOD," **REJOICE AND SING PRAISE**, ABINGDON PRESS, 1977)

(FOLLOWING THE SINGING, THEY ARE SEATED AT THE FRONT OF THE CHURCH)

LEADER: (contd) In good time God sent a hero named Moses. The people of Israel, our ancestors in the faith, were now in bondage in Egypt. They were forced to do hard, back-breaking work. They were beaten and starved. Moses, with God's help, led the people out of slavery in Egypt. God gave special laws to Moses, called the Ten Commandments. These were special rules by which the people were to live in order to please God and be his special people.

PROCESSION OF FIRST AND SECOND GRADERS: (IN ISRAELITE ROBES AND HEAD-DRESSES. ENTER TO MUSIC. THEY ASSEMBLE AT THE FRONT OF THE CHURCH AND SING. SUGGESTED SONG — "GO DOWN MOSES," **GOOD TIMES SONGBOOK**, ABINGDON PRESS, 1974)

(FOLLOWING THE SINGING, THEY ARE SEATED AT THE FRONT OF THE CHURCH)

LEADER: (contd) After the time of Moses, the people, our ancestors in the faith, began to settle in the Promised Land, the land of Canaan. This was a heroic time in the history of Israel, like our own pioneer period. The people of Israel divided into twelve tribes and scattered throughout the land. They settled down to an uneasy and uncertain existence beside Canaanite, walled cities. They were ruled by a judge. One of the greatest of these judges was the hero, Deborah. She successfully led her people against the great general Sisera, who had 900 chariots while the people of Israel had

LEADER: (contd) none. Miriam was another woman hero who was a prophet and leader of the people. Ester was a hero who was willing to give her life to save her people. Ruth also describes the period of the judges of Israel.

PROCESSION OF FIFTH AND SIXTH GRADERS: (ENTER TO MUSIC. AT THE FRONT OF THE CHURCH THEY SING AND DANCE WITH TAMBOURINES AND FINGER CYMBALS. SUGGESTED SONG — "WOMEN OF ISRAEL DANCE," **SIGNS, SONGS AND STORIES,** LITURGICAL CONFERENCE, INC.)

(FOLLOWING THE SINGING, THEY ARE SEATED AT THE FRONT OF THE CHURCH)

LEADER: (contd) The Golden Age for the people of Israel came during the time of our last hero, David. Under David, the twelve scattered tribes came together to form a single, powerful nation. Though David began as a simple shepherd boy, he became Israel's greatest king. He also wrote many of our loveliest psalms.

PROCESSION OF KINDERGARTENERS: (ENTER TO MUSIC DRESSED AS SHEPHERDS, SHEEP OR KINGS. THEY ASSEMBLE AT THE FRONT OF THE CHURCH AND SING. SUGGESTED SONG — "ONLY A BOY NAMED DAVID," **SING AND BE HAPPY SONGS FOR CHILDREN,** RODEHEAVER CO.)

(THESE CHILDREN CAN STAND IN PLACE AS THE LEADER SAYS HIS CLOSING REMARKS. THEY CAN FILE INTO THE PARADE AT THE APPROPRIATE TIME FROM THE FRONT OF THE CHURCH)

LEADER: We think it is important for us to learn these stories about our ancestors in the faith, our Old Testament heroes. We know that God is still calling people today to be heroes in the faith.

(ALL CHILDREN STAND AND SING THE ANCIENT ISRAELITE BENEDICTION, "SHALOM," **GENESIS SONGBOOK,** AGAPE PRESS, 1973)

(THEN ALL CHILDREN, LED BY THE BRASS BAND, FORM A PARADE, ENCIRCLING THE CONGREGATION, AND THEN MARCH TO A FELLOWSHIP HALL OR OUTDOORS AREA WHERE REFRESHMENTS MAY BE SERVED)

Mother's Day Open House

INTRODUCTION

Mother's Day is a Special Day in the life of many children and since the celebration began in the church, it is appropriate to celebrate it here. The celebration suggested includes many things that children love: art work, drama and parents visiting their rooms.

Each Church School room will present a play featuring a Biblical mother, and have an art display entitled, "My Mother," by members of the class.

PARTICIPANTS

Church School Classes, Parents
Teacher/Narrator (1 person or more)
Cast as indicated in each skit

MATERIALS

photographs
name cards
flower centerpieces
Bible verses on display
props as indicated in each skit
finished art displays using materials as indicated

PREPARATION

Encourage members of the congregation to bring photographs of their mothers. Those in the nostalgic dress of another period are especially good. Arrange the pictures on tables in the Fellowship Hall with a card telling the name of each mother pictured. It would be appropriate to center the tables with carnations or nosegay arrangements of old-fashioned flowers.

You may wish to have Bible verses on display. For example,

"Turn to me and have mercy on me. Strengthen me and save me because I serve you just as my mother did." (Psalms 86:16)

"I remember the sincere faith you have, the kind of faith that your grandmother, Lois, and your mother, Eunice, also had." (2 Timothy 1:5)

Students will have to prepare their art displays ahead of the day of the presentation.

ORDER OF PROGRAM

Pre-School Play Story: Moses' Mother
Pre-School Art Display: Poster Pictures

Kindergarten Echo Pantomime: The Lost Coin
Kindergarten Art Display: "Who Lives in My House?"

1st and 2nd Grade Puppet Show: Samuel's Mother
1st and 2nd Grade Art Display: Puppets-on-a-Stick representing Mothers

3rd and 4th Grade Bible Story: "How Jesus Answered a Mother's Prayer"
3rd and 4th Grade Art Display: Tempra Pictures

5th and 6th Grade TV Show: History of Mother's Day
5th and 6th Grade Art Display: Material Pictures

Reception

PRESENTATION

TEACHER: We want to welcome all of our parents here today. This is a special day in our Church School. Boys and girls, can you tell me what day it is?

CHILDREN: Mother's Day.

TEACHER: We have many mothers with us here today, don't we, and some grandmothers?

One of our favorite stories from the Bible is about something very brave that a mother did and we want to tell you that story.

Pre-School

PLAY-STORY: MOSES' MOTHER

(CAST: CHILDREN AS REEDS, CHILDREN AS WATER, MOTHER, PRINCESS, NARRATOR)

(PROPS: BRANCHES, STREAMERS, DOLL, TAMBOURINE)

(THIS PLAY/STORY IS ONE IN WHICH ALL THE CHILDREN TAKE PART. IT SHOULD BE SPONTANEOUS AND FUN FOR THE CHILDREN. THE PRINCESS AND MOSES' MOTHER COULD BE COSTUMED. OTHER CHILDREN CARRY REEDS OR BLUE CREPE PAPER STREAMERS)

NARRATOR: Long ago in the land of Egypt there lived a wicked King who wanted to kill all the little baby boys. At that time a beautiful baby boy was born. His mother was very, very sad and wanted to save her baby.

We will show you what she did. Not far from her house was a river with reeds growing tall in it.

(SOME CHILDREN COME FORWARD HOLDING LARGE BRANCHES SUGGESTING REEDS — OR BULRUSHES. DRIED PALM BRANCHES FROM PALM SUNDAY WORK VERY WELL)

These are the bulrushes.

(OTHER CHILDREN COME FORWARD HOLDING STREAMERS OF BLUE CREPE PAPER)

And this is the water. What happens when the wind blows?

(CHILDREN AS BULRUSHES SWAY BACK AND FORTH, WAVING REEDS. CHILDREN AS WATER RAISE THEIR STREAMERS AND SHAKE THEM. COULD USE PIANO ACCOMPANI – MENT HERE)

NARRATOR: (contd) There in the water by the bulrushes, the mother hid the baby.

(ONE CHILD, ACTING AS THE MOTHER, COMES FORWARD AND PLACES A DOLL IN A BASKET AMONG THE WAVES AND BULRUSHES)

The water and the bulrushes did all they could to help hide the baby.

(CHILDREN LEAN OVER BASKET, TRYING TO HIDE IT)

And then, what do you suppose happened? Along came a Princess and discovered the baby.

(CHILD ACTING AS PRINCESS FINDS BASKET)

She took the baby home and raised him in her own palace and the baby's mother got to go along and help take care of him.

(CHILDREN CHANT FOLLOWING. TEACHER TAPS TAMBOURINE TO GIVE RHYTHM FOR CHANT)

WATER: Wáter, Wáter, rócked the báby. (SHAKE STREAMERS)

BULRUSHES: Réeds grew úp and hid him wéll. (CHILDREN, HOLDING REEDS OVER HEADS, SQUAT DOWN AND SLOWLY RISE)

ALL: Ánd his móther lóved and sáved him. Thát's the stóry the Bíble télls.

TEACHER: And boys and girls, what was the name of that baby that grew up to be a Bible hero?

CHILDREN: Moses.

— END OF SKIT —

ART DISPLAY: POSTER PICTURES (OF CHILDRENS' MOTHERS)
INSTRUCTIONS — Use large pieces of poster board. Cut round faces and paste on board. Cut out a supply of eyes, eyebrows, noses and mouths from construction paper. Let children choose and arrange the features on the face. Glue in place. Have yarn in a variety of colors for hair. Let children choose and arrange the hair. Glue in place. Label each picture with name of the Mother represented.

Kindergarten
TEACHER OR CHILD: Mothers help us in so many ways. They cheer us up when we are sad. They comfort us when we are afraid. They laugh with us when we are happy. They help us tie our shoes and learn to read and cook our favorite foods and sometimes they help us find things that are lost. Once Jesus told a story about a mother who found something that was lost. We are going to act out this story for you now — The Lost Coin: Luke 15:8-9.

(NOTE: The following Echo Pantomime sketch is a reprinted version of **The Lost Coin**, by Judy Gattis Smith, available in a collection called **Four Parables of Jesus**, an activity packet, from Contemporary Drama Service, Arthur Meriwether Inc. Copyright 1972, Arthur Meriwether Inc. Used by permission.)

ECHO PANTOMIME: THE LOST COIN*
(CAST: WOMAN/NARRATOR, WHOLE CLASS)
(SETTING: INSIDE OF AN IMAGINARY HOUSE)

NARRATOR: Once there was a woman with ten silver coins. Let's count them.

(ALL CHILDREN IN THE CLASS STAND BESIDE WOMAN/NARRATOR AND ECHO
HER MOTIONS. HERE THEY COUNT 1-10, TAKING COINS FROM HAND AND PLACING IN
AN INVISIBLE BOX)

She kept them very carefully in a box in her home.

(SCOOP UP COINS AND DROP IN BOX, PUT ON LID AND PLACE ON SHELF)

One day she took the box down from the shelf,

(REACH UP)

put it on the table and looked inside.

(PLACE ON TABLE AND LIFT LID)

One of her coins was missing! What did she do? She looked in the box.

(TURN BOX UPSIDE DOWN)

Her house, like homes in Jesus' day, had thick walls of clay, straw and stone. It was dark because
there were no windows. She went and opened the one entrance door,

(PUSH OPEN THE DOOR)

and looked inside the house

(LOOK ALL AROUND)

but, although it was daytime, the room was still too dark. She hurried to get her pottery oil lamp.
There was only one in her modest home.

(CARRY AN IMAGINARY LAMP)

Carefully she lit the wick,

(LIGHT WICK)

and held the lamp high.

(HOLD OVER HEAD)

Now the room was much lighter, but she still could not see the coin.

(SHAKE HEAD, "NO")

Her eye catches a glimmer of silver.

(LOOK AROUND QUICKLY AND POINT LEFT)

No, it is not the coin. Her lamp has illuminated the tiny metal "mezuzah" box nailed to the door's
frame. She places the lamp back on the lamp stand, where it can brighten the room.

* See note on preceding page.

(REPLACE LAMP)

She gets down her broom

(REACH UP AND GET BROOM DOWN)

and begins to sweep the room.

(SWEEPING MOTION)

At first she sweeps very slowly,

(SWEEP SLOWLY)

and then she sweeps faster.

(SWEEP FAST)

But always carefully looking.

(STOP AND LOOK AROUND)

No coin.

(SHAKE HEAD "NO")

She is very sad.

(HAND TO HEAD)

She calls her children to her.

(MOTION WITH HAND FOR THEM TO COME)

But they have not seen the coin.

(SHAKE HEAD "NO")

They go back to their playing. She looks under the table,

(BEND DOWN AND LOOK)

but no coin.

(SHAKE HEAD "NO")

She moves the chairs,

(MOTION OF MOVING CHAIRS)

but no coin.

(SHAKE HEAD NO)

She climbs the steps to the roof. The roof is flat and made of reeds and soil and covered with tile.

(STEP WITH FEET AS THOUGH CLIMBING)

She looks all around.

(LOOK AROUND, HAND TO FOREHEAD)

She stops for a moment on the roof to smell the good earth.

(BIG SNIFF)

She feels the cool breeze.

(LITTLE SHIVER)

It is here on the roof that she offers her evening heart offering,

(ARMS EXTENDED UPWARD)

and sometimes even sleeps here.

(SLEEP POSE)

But for now she must continue her search. She comes slowly back down the steps.

(SLOWER STEP MOTIONS)

She opens the door,

(PUSH DOOR WITH HAND)

and stands in the room thinking: Where can it be?

(HEAD BENT, HAND ON FOREHEAD)

She goes to the corner where the sleeping mats are stored. Carefully she unrolls them.

(TURN HANDS OVER IN ROLLING MOTION)

There is no coin.

(SHAKE HEAD "NO")

Suddenly she hears a sound.

(STOP AND LISTEN)

The Master of the Springs has just called loudly throughout the village that it is time to get fresh water.

(HAND AT SIDE OF MOUTH AS THOUGH CALLING)

The woman picks up a jar to place on her head, for water is scarce, and can only be drawn from the well at certain times of the day.

(PUT IMAGINARY JAR ON HEAD)

There, underneath the jar, shines the coin!

(HANDS RAISED IN JOY, HAPPINESS ON FACE)

She calls her children.

(MOTION WITH HANDS FOR THEM TO COME)

Her son is skipping rope.

(SKIPPING MOTIONS)

Quickly he comes.

(PUT DOWN A ROPE)

Her daughter is bouncing a ball.

(PANTOMIME BOUNCING A BALL)

Quickly she comes. The mother shows them the coin.

(HOLD COIN HIGH)

All together they count the coins.

(COUNT 1-10)

The son gets the wood flute and begins to play

(PANTOMIME FLUTE PLAYING)

and everyone is happy because the lost coin has been found.

NARRATOR: This parable shows how God rejoices at a renewed relationship with a person that is lost. Isn't it interesting that Jesus makes the analogue to God a woman?

— END OF ECHO PANTAMIME —

ART DISPLAY: "WHO LIVES IN MY HOUSE?"
INSTRUCTIONS — Cut out pattern of a house, one for each child.

Write "Who Lives in My House?" in the roof area. Let children look through magazines for pictures that remind them in action and features of their own Mothers. Have them cut the pictures out and paste them in the house. Label each picture with the Mother's name and the student's name.

1st and 2nd Grade
PUPPET PLAY: "SAMUEL'S MOTHER"
(CAST: NARRATOR, PUPPETEERS)
(PROPS: PUPPETS OF TEMPLE, ELKANAH, HANNAH, SAMUEL, ELI, COATS, CHILDREN)

(INSTRUCTIONS FOR MAKING THESE PUPPETS AND A SIMPLE STAGE ARE FOUND
IN THE ART DISPLAY INSTRUCTIONS FOLLOWING)

NARRATOR: In the land of Israel there lived a man named Elkanah.

(PUPPET APPEARS)

This man feared God and every year he went to Shiloh to take an offering to the Temple there.

(TEMPLE-ON-A-STICK APPEARS)

He did not go alone, but took his family with him and they worshipped God together.

(HANNAH APPEARS)

But Hannah, Elkanah's wife, was very unhappy because God had never given her a child.

(HANNAH PUPPET WEEPS. SOUNDS FROM BACKSTAGE)

Even though Elkanah loved her dearly and gave her much honor, still Hannah would not be comforted.

(LOUDER WEEPING)

NARRATOR: (contd) One year when she went with her husband to offer sacrifices at Shiloh, she prayed and asked God to give her a baby boy.

(ELKANAH EXITS. HANNAH BOWS DOWN IN FRONT OF TEMPLE)

She promised to lend the little boy back to God if only he would answer her prayer.

(HANNAH EXITS)

God did answer Hannah's prayer. Before another year passed, a baby boy was born. And Hannah named him Samuel which means "Asked of God."

(SAMUEL PUPPET APPEARS)

When Samuel was still a very young child, Hannah took him to Shiloh.

(HANNAH AND SAMUEL PUPPET WALK TO SHILOH)

There she brought him to the high priest whose name was Eli.

(ELI PUPPET APPEARS)

Hannah told Eli how she had prayed for this child and how she had promised to lend him to the Lord as long as he should live. Now she wanted Samuel to live near the tabernacle and learn how to help the high priest.

(HANNAH PUPPET MOVES AS SHE TALKS. OTHERS FREEZE)

Eli promised to take care of her little boy and teach him to serve God.

(ELI PUPPET MOVES, OTHERS FREEZE)

(HANNAH EXITS, THEN ELI AND SAMUEL EXIT)

Every year after this, when the time came for Elkanah to offer his sacrifices at Shiloh, Hannah came too, and every year she brought a new coat for her little boy.

(ELKANAH, HANNAH AND COAT-ON-A-STICK APPEAR)

(PUPPETS MOVE ACROSS STAGE TO TEMPLE, EXIT AND COME AGAIN WITH A LARGER COAT-ON-A-STICK. THIS MAY BE DONE SEVERAL TIMES)

How happy Hannah was to see Samuel every year.

(SAMUEL PUPPET APPEARS)

How thankfully she listened to the many things little Samuel was learning to do.

(SAMUEL PUPPET MOVES AS TALKING)

Her heart was very glad because God had answered her prayers.

(HANNAH PUPPET DANCES FOR JOY)

Samuel grew up to be a great prophet of God, and God blessed Elkanah and Hannah with other children besides Samuel.

(OTHER CHILDREN PUPPETS APPEAR — AS MANY AS YOU LIKE)

— END OF PLAY —

TEACHER: This ends our Bible story. Now we would like for you to meet our Mothers as we see them.

(PUPPETS-ON-A-STICK, REPRESENTING THE CHILDRENS' MOTHERS, POP UP, ONE AT A TIME. CHILD INTRODUCES HIS OR HER MOTHER: "THIS IS MY MOTHER, MARY JONES," ETC.)

ART DISPLAY: PUPPETS-ON-A-STICK REPRESENTING MOTHERS
INSTRUCTIONS — Both the Mother's Day Art Display and the characters for the play, "Samuel's Mother" will be puppets-on-a-stick. Puppets-on-a-stick are figures drawn on cardboard, decorated with crayons or paint, cut out and thumbtacked to a ruler.

Though these puppets lack the freedom of movement of hand puppets, they are fun because the scenery and props can also be on-a-stick. In this play, the temple and Samuel's coats are examples. The main movement of the puppets will be up and down movement as they talk and do simple action movements like walk across the stage or dance for joy.

The stage for the puppet show can be a long table draped with a sheet. The children crouch behind the table and try to conceal both the sticks and their hands as they work the puppets.

Besides the characters in the play, the children should make puppets-on-a-stick to represent their Mothers for the presentation at the end of the play.

3rd and 4th Grade
BIBLE STORY: "HOW JESUS ANSWERED A MOTHER'S PRAYER"
(CAST: CHILD 1, 2, 3, 4, 5, 6, 7, 8, 9, 10)
(PROPS: SHEET WITH STORY TITLE, PICTURES)

(THIS STORY USES PICTURES MADE BY THE CHILDREN. INSTRUCTIONS FOR MAKING THESE PICTURES ARE FOUND IN THE ART DISPLAY INSTRUCTIONS FOLLOWING. THEY ILLUSTRATE THE PART OF THE STORY EACH CHILD TELLS. ALL CHILDREN LINE UP IN FRONT OF THE ROOM IN ORDER. THEY SPEAK THEIR PART AND SHOW THEIR PICTURES. ONCE UP, ALL PICTURES ARE HELD UP UNTIL THE STORY IS COMPLETED)

CHILD 1: The Bible story we would like to share with you this morning is about how Jesus answered a mother's prayer. It is found in the Bible in Matthew 15:21-29 and in Mark 7:24-30.

(HOLDS UP SHEET WITH STORY TITLE)

CHILD 2: Near the land of Galilee was a small country called Phoenicia. The people who lived in this land did not worship God, but worshipped idols.

(HOLDS UP PICTURE OF IDOL)

CHILD 3: One day Jesus wanted to be alone with his disciples. So he took them for a long walk. They walked all the way to Phoenicia.

(HOLDS UP A PICTURE ILLUSTRATING THIS)

CHILD 4: Living in this country was one poor mother whose heart was very sad because she had

CHILD 4: (contd) a little girl who was very sick.

(HOLDS UP PICTURE)

CHILD 5: The mother had heard about Jesus and how he could heal the sick, so when she heard he was in Phoenicia, she ran to find him.

(HOLDS UP PICTURE)

CHILD 6: The disciples were angry with the woman for bothering Jesus.

(HOLDS UP PICTURE)

CHILD 7: But Jesus is alway touched when he hears the cry of one in need. He listened to the woman's story.

(HOLDS UP PICTURE)

CHILD 8: But since she was a Gentile, he wanted to test her faith, so he said, "I am not sent to the Gentiles, but to the lost children of Israel. And it is not fitting to take children's bread and throw it to the dogs."

(HOLDS UP PICTURE)

CHILD 9: The proud Jews called the Gentiles "dogs," but this mother was now willing to be called even a dog if only the great Healer would help her child. So she said, "I know it is true that children's bread should not be given to dogs, yet we know that dogs eat of the crumbs that fall from the table."

(HOLDS UP PICTURE)

CHILD 10: Jesus was greatly pleased when he heard her wise reply, and he said, "O mother, great is your faith in me! You shall receive what you have asked. Go back home. Your child is well."

(HOLDS UP PICTURE)

ALL: Jesus had answered a mother's prayer.

— END OF BIBLE STORY —

ART DISPLAY: TEMPRA PICTURES
INSTRUCTIONS — Each child in the class should do both a picture of "My Mother" and an illustration for his or her portion of the Bible story to be presented to the parents.

Use tempra paints on drawing paper for the pictures. Mount the pictures on cardboard which has been covered with colorful fabrics. This results in pictures with bright, colorful frames.

Have the pictures of the Mothers arranged for all to see, with a label to tell the name of the Mother and the student.

5th and 6th Grade
TV SHOW: HISTORY OF MOTHER'S DAY
(CAST: HOST, ANNA, PEOPLE TO ASK QUESTIONS)
(PROPS: TABLES AND CHAIRS TO SUGGEST A TV SHOW SET)
(THIS SKIT IS TO BE LIKE A TV TALK SHOW. LET THE CLASS CHOOSE A FAVORITE

CELEBRITY HOST TO PATTERN THE HOST OF THEIR SHOW AFTER. BEGIN THE PROGRAM AS HE OR SHE WOULD BEGIN THE SHOW)

HOST: Today we are going to be interviewing a famous person to try to find out something about this celebration of Mother's Day. Our special guest is Mrs. Anna Jarvis. She is credited with being the real founder of Mother's Day in our country.

Welcome Mrs. Jarvis. Please be seated and tell us a little about your background.

ANNA: I was born in 1864 in Grafton, West Virginia.

HOST: That was just after the Civil War.

ANNA: Yes, it was. The War ended right after I was born, but when I was growing up there was still much hatred between families. Because, you see, in West Virginia, sometimes one brother had fought on the Northern Side while another brother had fought for the South.

HOST: That would cause problems.

ANNA: Yes, and so many times I remember my mother saying if the family honored their mother, the brothers would forget about fighting.

HOST: Is that where you got the idea for Mother's Day?

ANNA: I suppose it was. I can remember wishing, as a young child, that sometime, somewhere, someone would start a Mother's Day.

HOST: Did you think it would be you?

ANNA: No, I didn't at that time. I went to college and later moved to Philadelphia. It was when my mother died that I decided to be that someone. I promised I would try to begin a Mother's Day for people everywhere.

HOST: I wonder if there are questions from the audience?

QUESTION 1: How did you go about it? Was it easy?

ANNA: It was easier than you might suppose. I began in the church. I asked the minister in Grafton, West Virginia, if he would hold a special Mother's Day service. And he did on May 12, 1907.

HOST: And that was the beginning? In a local church just like ours?

ANNA: Yes, and then the next year I persuaded the people of Philadelphia to celebrate the second Sunday in May as a special day for Mothers. After that it just seemed to catch fire. People all over the country began to celebrate.

HOST: And then you could sit back and relax.

ANNA: O no. My work was just beginning. I gave up my job and spent all my time working for Mother's Day. I wrote letters to people all over the world — to presidents and ministers, to congressmen and kings. By 1909 every state in the country was celebrating this special day.

HOST: In only two years you were able to accomplish that?

ANNA: Yes, but my greatest accomplishment came five years later. On May 9, 1914, President Woodrow Wilson signed a proclamation proclaiming the second Sunday in May as Mother's Day in every state.

HOST: You certainly carried out your promise.

ANNA: No. I still had work to do. Next I organized an International Mother's Day Association and my idea spread to more than 40 countries.

HOST: Is there another question from the audience?

QUESTION 2: How did you convince people of your idea?

ANNA: I just explained to them that the purpose was "to honor the best mother who ever lived — your mother."

QUESTION 3: Did the idea of wearing flowers on Mother's Day originate with you?

ANNA: Yes, it did. As a little girl I helped my mother weed the flower garden in front of our house. It was filled with lovely white carnations — her favorite flower. At first everyone wore white carnations. Later I suggested that people whose mothers were living should wear pink carnations.

QUESTION 4: Which are the other countries that celebrate Mother's Day?

ANNA: Denmark, Japan, Finland, Italy, Turkey, Australia and Belgium are a few of them. In these countries, boys and girls celebrate on the second Sunday in May just as we do.

Other countries have different dates. Norway celebrates in February, Argentina in October, in Lebanon and South Africa it is early in the Spring. In Yugoslavia, it is right before Christmas.

QUESTION 5: Had anyone ever thought of the idea of Mother's Day before?

ANNA: There was an interesting celebration that took place way back during the Middle Ages. Most boys and girls had to leave home to earn money. Boys worked as apprentices to learn a trade, girls worked as servants. They were allowed only one holiday a year. On the 4th Sunday in Lent the children went home to see their mothers. It became known as Mothering Sunday.

QUESTION 6: Has there ever been a Mother's Day stamp?

ANNA: Yes. In 1934 there was a special Mother's Stamp issued. It showed the famous portrait of Whistler's Mother with a bowl of carnations added and it was printed with the words, "In Memory and in Honor of the Mothers of America."

HOST: Our time is about up. Is there anything else you would like to tell us, Mrs. Jarvis?

ANNA: Only that this idea would not have been possible without the help of the church. Both our Old and New Testaments speak with reverence about mothers.

HOST: Thank you, Mrs. Anna Jarvis. And thank you, members of the audience.

— END OF TV SHOW —

ART DISPLAY: MATERIAL PICTURES
INSTRUCTIONS — Have each student choose a piece of material that reminds him or her of his or her Mother. The teacher can have a large supply of scraps of all textures and colors on hand, or a student may bring scraps from an actual dress of his or her mother. These pieces of material are mounted on poster board for a novel, interpretive illustration of "My Mother."

Reception

All may join together for refreshments after all the classes have presented their skits and art displays. This may be held in the Fellowship Hall. Everyone will have a chance to view all the pictures of the mothers and grandmothers brought in and put on display by the members of the congregation.

SUMMER
JUNE/JULY/AUGUST

SPECIAL DAYS IN SUMMER

Pentecost is that season in the Church Year where we dramatize in word, act and symbol the receiving of the gift of the Holy Spirit. The sanctuary, with a special children's liturgy, is a meaningful setting for this Special Day.

And then — Summer. In summer our pace in the Church School often changes. We are more unstructured as children come and go on vacations. It's a good time to try something different. What about a pageant for Father's Day? Who said Christmas is the only time for a Church pageant? And are churches the only ones that can celebrate anniversaries? What about a joyful Church School birthday party?

And then, just before school starts, (because this is the time children think of a new year beginning) have a special service welcoming new members of the Church School. Entwine their past with yours and begin together to plan another glorious year of Special Days.

A Children's Pentecost Liturgy

INTRODUCTION

This is a children's liturgy for the celebration of Pentecost, to be used in the church sanctuary. It combines giving thanks for the gift of the Holy Spirit with recognition of the fruits it brings us.

PARTICIPANTS

Reader for Introit
Sound-Effects Choir
Two Readers for Ezekiel Story
Eight Children with "Fruits of the Spirit"
Four Trumpeteers

MATERIALS

tree branch
apple slices, baskets
gourds, tambourine, drum for Sound-Effects Choir
8 poster board apples with words printed on them

SOURCES FOR MUSIC SUGGESTIONS

"Come Thou Almight King" — found in most hymnals
"Breathe on Me Breathe of God" — the Methodist Hymnal, No. 133.
"Spirit of Faith Come Down" — the Methodist Hymnal, No. 137.
"Holy, Holy, Holy" — found in most hymnals
"God of Our Fathers" — the Methodist Hymnal, No. 552.
"I'm Gonna Sing when the Spirit Says Sing" — **Good Times Songbook**, James Leisy, Abingdon
      Press, 1974.
"Praise to the Living God" — the Methodist Hymnal, No. 30.
"Spirit of God Descend Upon My Heart" — the Methodist Hymnal, No. 138.
"They'll Know We Are Christians by Our Love" — **Genesis Songbook**, Agape Press, 1973.

LITURGY

Trumpeting in Pentecost

Four trumpeteers stand facing the four points on the compass. Each in turn plays a Pentecost hymn. Suggested hymns are: Trumpet 1: "Come Thou Almight King," Trumpet 2: "Breathe on Me Breath of God," Trumpet 3: "Spirit of Faith Come Down," and Trumpet 4: "Holy, Holy, Holy." (See music sources on page 103.)

Introit

MINISTER: (Psalms 24:7-10) Fling wide the gates. Open the ancient doors, And the great king will come in.

CHILD: Who is this great king?

CONGREGATION: He is the Lord, strong and mighty, the Lord, victorious in battle.

MINISTER: Fling wide the gates. Open the ancient doors. And the great king will come in.

CHILD: Who is this great king?

CONGREGATION: The triumphant Lord. He is the Great King.

HYMN: "God of our Fathers" (THE METHODIST HYMNAL, NO. 552. WITH ORGAN, CHOIR AND TRUMPET ACCOMPANIMENT, IF DESIRED)

MINISTER: Today we come together to celebrate Pentecost. We thank God for the coming of the Holy Spirit, for the beginning of the church and we earnestly seek the continuing presence of the Spirit with us in the ongoing life of the church today. Let us hear the ancient story:

First the promises of Jesus. (John 14:15) If you love me you will obey my commandments. I will ask the Father and he will give you another Helper who will stay with you forever. He is the Holy Spirit who reveals the truth about God.

CONGREGATION: Come Holy Spirit. Come today.

MINISTER: I have told you this while I am still with you, the Helper, the Holy Spirit, whom the father will send in my name, will teach you everything and make you remember all that I have told you.

CONGREGATION: Come Holy Spirit. Come today.

MINISTER: And Jesus kept his promise. (Acts 2:1-4) When the day of Pentecost came, all the believers were gathered together in one place. Suddenly, there was a noise from the sky which sounded like a strong wind blowing, and it filled the whole house where they were sitting. Then they saw what looked like tongues of fire which spread out and touched each person there. They were all filled with the Holy Spirit and began to talk in other languages as the Spirit enabled them to speak.

CONGREGATION: Come Holy Spirit. Come today.

MINISTER: What an exciting time that must have been. To try to capture the feeling of that day, let us sing the spiritual, "I'm Gonna Sing when the Spirit says Sing." You may clap if you wish.

HYMN: "I'm Gonna Sing When the Spirit Says Sing" (**GOOD TIMES SONGBOOK**, ABINGDON PRESS, 1974)

MINISTER: Often today we feel no rushing winds, no tongues of fire. Isaac Watts captured this feeling for us in these words:

> Come Holy Spirit, heavenly Dove, With all thy quickening powers,
> Kindle a flame of sacred love, In these cold hearts of ours.
>
> Look how we grovel here below, Fond of these earthly toys,
> Our souls, how heavily they go, To reach eternal joys.
>
> In vain we tune our formal songs, In vain we strive to rise,
> Hosannas languish on our tongues, And our devotion dies.
>
> And shall we then forever live, At this poor dying rate?
> Our love so faint, so cold to thee, And thine to us, so great!
>
> Come Holy Spirit, heavenly Dove, With all thy quickening powers,
> Come shed abroad a Saviour's love, And that shall kindle ours.

Ezekiel Story

MINISTER: Can a church that is luke-warm come alive with the Spirit? Can our love so faint and cold respond to the great love of God? A group of boys and girls will interpret an ancient story for us from the book of Ezekiel in the Old Testament.

(CHILDREN FORM A SOUND-EFFECTS CHOIR)

READER 1: (Ezekiel 37, King James Version) The hand of the Lord was upon me and carried me out in the spirit of the Lord and set me down in the midst of the valley which was full of bones. And caused me to pass by them round about; and, behold, there were very many in the open valley and lo they were very dry.

(CHOIR SHAKES GOURD RATTLES)

and he said to me:

READER 2: Son of man, can these bones live?

READER 1: And I answered, O Lord God, thou knowest.

READER 2: Prophesy upon these bones and say to them, O ye dry bones, hear the word of the Lord. Thus saith the Lord God unto these bones. Behold I will cause breath to enter into you and ye shall live. And I will lay sinews upon you and will bring up flesh upon you and cover you with skin and put breath in you and ye shall live and ye shall know that I am the Lord.

READER 1: So I prophesied as I was commanded, and as I prophesied, there was a noise and behold, a shaking and the bones came together, bone to his bone.

(CHOIR: SHAKE GOURD RATTLES AND TAMBOURINES, AND GIVE DRUM ROLL)

READER 1: And when I beheld, lo, the sinews and the flesh came up upon them, and the skin covered them above but there was no breath in them. Then he said to me:

READER 2: Prophesy unto the wind, prophesy, Son of man, and say to the wind, Thus saith the Lord God. Come from the four winds, O breath, and breathe upon these slain that they may live.

READER 1: So I prophesied as he commanded me and the breath came into them and they lived.

(CHOIR MAKES BLOWING WIND SOUND)

And they stood upon their feet, an exceeding great army.

(CHOIR STANDS AND MARCHES IN PLACE. AFTER A FEW MOMENTS THE CONGREGATION IS MOTIONED TO STAND)

Then he said unto me:

READER 2: Son of man, these bones are the whole House of Israel: behold, they say, Our bones are dried and our hope is lost: we are cut off from our parts. Therefore prophesy and say unto them. Thus saith the Lord God, Behold, O my people. I will open your graves and cause you to come up out of your graves and bring you into the land of Israel. And ye shall know that I am the Lord, when I have opened your graves, O my people, and brought you up out of your graves. And shall put my spirit in you and ye shall live and I shall place you in your own land: then shall ye know that I the Lord have spoken it and performed it, saith the Lord.

HYMN: "Praise to the Living God" (THE METHODIST HYMNAL, NO. 30)

MINISTER: And how do we know when we have received the Spirit, in our church and in our personal lives? (CONGREGATION IS SEATED)

Fruits of the Spirit

MINISTER: (contd) Again the Bible gives us wisdom. Galatians 5 tells us that there are fruits of the Spirit, produce that is a result of the Spirit dwelling within us.

What are the fruits of the Spirit?

(A TREE BRANCH IS ON THE ALTAR OR ON THE FLOOR BESIDE THE ALTAR)

(EIGHT CHILDREN COME FORWARD, ONE AT A TIME, CARRYING A LARGE APPLE CUT FROM RED POSTER PAPER, BEARING ONE OF THE WORDS OF THE FRUITS OF THE SPIRIT. THE WORDS SHOULD BE LARGE ENOUGH FOR THE CONGREGATION TO READ)

(AFTER EACH CHILD SAYS THE WORD PRINTED ON HIS OR HER APPLE, THE APPLE IS HUNG ON THE TREE BRANCH)

CHILD 1: Love

CHILD 2: Joy

CHILD 3: Peace

CHILD 4: Kindness

CHILD 5: Goodness

CHILD 6: Faithfulness

CHILD 7: Humility

CHILD 8: Self Control

(CHILDREN RETURN TO THEIR SEATS)

MINISTER: Let us meditate on these fruits of the Spirit. Search your own hearts and see if these traits rule your life, remembering also these words from Galatians 6:7-10:   A person will reap exactly what he plants. If he plants in the field of his natural desires, from it he will gather the harvest of death. If he plants in the field of the Spirit, from the Spirit he will gather the harvest of eternal life. So let us not become tired of doing good; for if we do not give up, the time will come when we will reap the harvest. So then, as often as we have the chance, we should do good to everyone, and especially to those who belong to our family in the faith.

Passing Out of Apples

MINISTER: (contd) As an act of dedication our ushers are passing among you baskets of apples. Take a piece and eat and pray that the fruits of the Spirit may become the fruits of your life.

(USHERS PASS APPLES AS ORGAN PLAYS HYMNS. SUGGESTED: "SPIRIT OF GOD DESCEND UPON MY HEART," FROM THE METHODIST HYMNAL, NO. 138)

(WHEN ALL HAVE PARTAKEN, THE MINISTER SAYS)

Thank you Father, for the apple seeds and for all the seeds of the Spirit that are waiting to come to life in us. May your Spirit fill our church and our lives. Amen.

HYMN: "They'll Know We Are Christians by Our Love" (**GENESIS SONGBOOK**, AGAPE PRESS, 1973. ON VERSE 2, CHILDREN WHO CARRIED APPLES AND MINISTER PROCESS OUT. THE REST OF THE CONGREGATION THEN BEGINS TO RECESS, FROM THE FRONT PEWS BACK. BEGIN AGAIN AT VERSE 1 IF NEEDED, UNTIL ALL HAVE RECESSED)

Church School Birthday Party

INTRODUCTION

What are we really celebrating when we celebrate birthdays? Is it not growth? Is it not the past, the present and the future? Then why not a Church School birthday party? Many churches celebrate their beginnings on their anniversaries, but that is often too far removed from the Church School. Following is an intergenerational celebration of the Church School.

PARTICIPANTS

Leader

6 Card Readers

Early Teacher or Historian

Minister

Church School Classes and Teachers

MATERIALS

student pictures, construction paper flowers

Bible verse cards

a history of the church school

ladder

colorful paper with yarn attached

pencils and pens

materials as listed for making gifts

birthday cake

SOURCES FOR MUSIC SUGGESTIONS

"O God Our Help in Ages Past" — the Methodist Hymnal, No. 28.

"A Charge to Keep I Have" — the Methodist Hymnal, No. 150.

"Jacob's Ladder" — the Methodist Hymnal, No. 287.

"Come Christians Join to Sing" — the Methodist Hymnal, No. 77.

PREPARATION

Decorate the Fellowship Hall or a large classroom with pictures of all the children in the Church School. School pictures are good, or take your own shots. Put these pictures in the center of large construction paper flowers with the caption, "Church School is blooming."

PARTY LITURGY

OPENING SONG: "Happy Birthday"

LEADER: We have come together today to celebrate the birthday of our Church School. Hear our Biblical mandates.

Card Reading

(PASS OUT CARDS WITH THE FOLLOWING BIBLE VERSES ON THEM. PERSONS STAND AND READ)

READER 1: We are fellow workers for God. You are God's field, God's building. (1 Corinthians 3:9 Revised Standard Version)

READER 2: The harvest is plentiful but the laborers are few; pray the Lord to send out laborers into his harvest. (Luke 10:2 Revised Standard Version)

READER 3: Take heed to yourself and to your teaching; hold to that, for by so doing you will save both yourself and your hearers. (1 Timothy 4:16 Revised Standard Version)

READER 4: Train up a child in the way he should go, and when he is old he will not depart from it. (Proverbs 22:6 Revised Standard Version)

READER 5: Let the children come to me and do not hinder them, for to such belongs the Kingdom of God. (Luke 18:16 Revised Standard Version)

READER 6: Not that we are sufficient of ourselves to claim anything as coming from us; our sufficiency is from God. (2 Corinthians 3:5 Revised Standard Version)

History

LEADER: Let's begin where birthdays begin — at birth — the birth of our Church School.

(A CHURCH HISTORIAN OR AN EARLY TEACHER GIVES INPUT ON HOW OLD YOUR CHURCH SCHOOL IS, THE DATE IT WAS ORGANIZED, WHEN THE EDUCATIONAL FACILITIES WERE BUILT. IF POSSIBLE, HE OR SHE SHARES PICTURES FROM THAT EARLY BEGINNING)

(IF ANY OF THE FIRST TEACHERS ARE PRESENT, THEY ARE INTRODUCED AND GIVEN A FEW MOMENTS TO RECALL EVENTS FROM THE EARLY DAYS IN YOUR CHURCH SCHOOL. FOR EXAMPLE, THE NUMBER OF CLASSES WITH WHICH THE CHURCH SCHOOL BEGAN AND THE EARLY ENROLLMENT FIGURES WOULD BE INTERESTING)

HYMN: "O God Our Help In Ages Past" (THE METHODIST HYMNAL, NO. 28)

MINISTER: Heavenly Father, hear our prayers of gratitude for those who had the courage to begin this Church School. We remember the time and the prayers and the tears that went into its beginning. Make us worthy of this inheritance.

LEADER: With gratitude for the past, we look now at the present. Will our current teachers please stand, give us their names, their classes and its current enrollment?

(TEACHERS DO SO)

LEADER: (contd) God always works and speaks through persons. These are the persons in our classrooms through whom God will speak to our boys and girls.

We want to learn more about our teachers because each of us is different and unique.

Identification Activity

(THIS ACTIVITY MAY BE DONE WITH THE WHOLE GROUP, IF THE GROUP IS NOT TOO LARGE, OR IT CAN BE DONE WITH ONLY TEACHERS, PAST AND PRESENT)

LEADER: (contd) I am going to list several pairs of words and each of you must decide with which half of each pair you identify more. You will then come and stand either on one side of the room or the other, affirming your choices. Discuss with the persons there the reason for your choices, and then share your thoughts with the whole group. Are you more like:

> a babbling brook or a placid lake
> New York City or Colorado
> an electric typewriter or a quill pen
> a prophet or a shepherd

(TEACHERS TAKE PART IN THIS ACTIVITY, THEN RETURN TO THEIR SEATS)

MINISTER: We thank God for the diversity of talents and personalities that are our teachers.

HYMN: "A Charge to Keep I Have" (THE METHODIST HYMNAL, NO. 150)

Questions

(IN PLACE OF, OR IN ADDITION TO, THE ACTIVITY PRECEDING THE ABOVE HYMN, YOU MAY WISH TO HAVE A CONTEST AMONG THE GROUP. AS QUESTIONS SUCH AS THE FOLLOWING)

1. Who has been attending Church School the longest?
2. Who has the longest record of unbroken attendance?
3. Who is the newest member of our Church School?
4. Which is the largest class?

LEADER: We have looked at the past and the present, but what about the future? Birthday time is always a time for wishes. What is your wish for our Church School for the future?

The Wishing Ladder

(A LADDER IS BROUGHT IN)

LEADER: (contd) This is a "wishing ladder." We hope we are climbing to better and better things. Will each of you write a wish for our Church School on the pieces of paper we will pass out, and hang your wish on our wishing ladder?

(COLORFUL PIECES OF PAPER WITH YARN ATTACHED FOR HANGING ON LADDER ARE GIVEN TO EACH PERSON PRESENT. THEY WRITE THEIR WISHES AND HANG THEM ON THE LADDER. WISHES MAY BE SHARED ALOUD OR NOT)

SONG: "Jacob's Ladder" (THE METHODIST HYMNAL, NO. 287)

LEADER: The past, the present and the future are all important parts of our Church School. But what is a birthday party without gifts? We want to divide into three groups now and each create a gift for the Church School.

Making Gifts

GROUP 1 — CREATE A FLAG FOR OUR CHURCH SCHOOL

(INSTRUCTIONS) Some principles of flags: A flag should be designed with certain established principles in mind. The simpler the design, the better it is. Colors should be arranged in stark contrasts. The figures or symbols on the colors should be easily legible. Keep in mind that a flag should have maximum visibility and immediate identification.

What are the ideals and goals of your Church School? What is a symbol or idea that conveys these goals? First, decide as a group on your design and colors. Then have a variety of colors of felt, scissors, pencils, rulers and glue on hand to create your design. Have a pole on which to display your flag.

GROUP 2 — CREATE A MOTTO FOR YOUR CHURCH SCHOOL

(INSTRUCTIONS) A motto is a brief sentence, phrase or single word used to express a principle, goal or ideal. Decide as a group on a motto for your Church School. If your church has a motto, you might discuss the group's understanding of that motto. When the group has agreed, write the motto on a long strip of paper. Roll the two ends on dowel sticks like a scroll.

GROUP 3 — DEVELOP A TIME CAPSULE FOR YOUR CHURCH SCHOOL

(INSTRUCTIONS) Your group will be writing down various items that tell something about your Church School at the present moment. These ideas are preserved for a future when someone will open the capsule. The future will get a glimpse of the past.

Each member of the group lists five items which he or she thinks should be included in the capsule. The members of the group share their ideas and decide on a final list of ten items. The members draw or symbolize these items and place them in a box.

When the three groups have finished, they come together and share what they have created.

Parade

(INSTRUCTIONS) As a final act of celebration, the entire group parades with the flag, motto and time capsule around the room to music. Suggested marching hymn; "Come Christians Join to Sing" from the Methodist Hymnal, No. 77. Or you may use another favorite hymn of your Church School.

The group ends up at a location where there is a large birthday cake. The flag and motto are displayed in a prominent place in the Church School and the time capsule is stored for a future opening.

Father's Day Pageant — Story of Joseph

INTRODUCTION

A pageant is a special show in which lots of people usually take small parts and just a few take big parts. In this pageant, the Narrator has the main speaking part. He or she stands at one side of the play area and tells the audience what is going on.

The other single actor in this pageant is Joseph. He has no speaking part, but he must have two costumes: a coat of many colors and the robe of a high Egyptian official.

Pageants usually feature interesting things to look at and that will be the secret of your successful pageant: beautiful costumes, large groups of people moving in interesting ways and special scenery effects.

PARTICIPANTS

Narrator, Joseph
Minister, Congregation
2 year olds as grain
3-4 year olds as stars, sun, moon
5 year olds as bricks
6-7 year olds for Ishmaelite procession
8-9 year olds for People of the World
10-11 year olds for card choir

MATERIALS

coat of many colors, Egyptian robe
7 sets of cards as described (SEE PREPARATION)
costumes and props for children as indicated in the script

SOURCES FOR MUSIC SUGGESTIONS

"Faith of Our Fathers" — the Methodist Hymnal, No. 151.
"Zum Gali Gali Gali" — **The Good Times Songbook**, James Leisy, Abingdon Press, 1974.
"Hymn to Joy" — Beethoven, found in the hymn, "Joyful, Joyful, We Adore Thee" — the Methodist Hymnal, No. 38.
"Doxology" also known as "Praise God from Whom All Blessings Flow" — found in most hymnals

PREPARATION

The entire Church School can work on this pageant — each class working separately. They will only need one rehearsal for putting the whole show together.

2 year olds are "grain." They should work on the interesting costumes, the simple song and the simple movements indicated in the script.

3 and 4 year olds are stars, sun and moon. They too should work on the interesting costumes, the simple song and the simple movements indicated in the script.

5 year olds are bricks. They should work on interesting props or costumes, the simple song and the stage movements indicated in the script.

6 and 7 year olds can form the Ishmaelite procession. They should work on costumes and props, learn the folk song and practice processing down the aisle of the church in an interesting manner as indicated in the script.

8 and 9 year olds can form the People of the World procession. They can use creative costumes, flags or banners from other countries, learn a song and work on processing in an interesting manner as indicated in the script.

10 and 11 year olds can form the card choir. They remain in the front of the church the entire time. There are 7 card sets. They will need a director and need to practice a number of times for smoothness. They will form the special scenery effects as indicated in the script. Card sets are:

    Set 1: Colors (8 colors, variable number of cards)
    Set 2: Brother's Names (11 cards)
    Set 3: Words of the Father — Sad (10 cards, on black cards if possible)
    Set 4: Egyptian palace — grid picture (12 cards)
    Set 5: Blank cards to be waved when saying, "Go! Go!" (variable number of cards)
    Set 6: Words of the Father — Happy (10 cards)
    Set 7: Acrostic to form words: Praise God (9 cards)

These are explained in more detail in the script at the appropriate places. Set 2 is repeated between Sets 4 and 5.

Divide the card sets among the Card Choir members so that they can be raised and lowered smoothly during the narration without too much fumbling by the choir members. Depending on the size of the choir, the cards may be allocated differently.

For example, for Card Set 1, each member could hold a different color if there were 8 members. Several members could hold each color if multiple cards for each color were made. With more members, the choir could be divided into sections so that different sections hold up different sets. In this case, only 8 members of the total might hold up Card Set 1. Fewer members, of course, can hold multiple cards from any of the sets.

PAGEANT

MINISTER: We want to welcome all of you here today and especially our fathers.

Introit

MINISTER: (contd) The lines are fallen unto me in pleasant places, yea I have a goodly heritage. (Psalms 16:6 King James Version)

CONGREGATION: Our fathers put their trust in you and you saved them. (Psalms 22:4)

WOMEN: With our own ears we have heard it, O God. Our fathers have told us about it. About the great things you did in their time, in the days long ago. (Psalms 44:1)

MEN: He gave laws to the people of Israel and commandments to the descendants of Jacob. He instructed our fathers to teach his law to their children. So that the next generation might learn them and in turn should tell their children. In this way they also put their trust in God, and not forget what he has done but always obey his commandments. (Psalms 78:5-7)

HYMN: (ALL) "Faith of Our Fathers" (THE METHODIST HYMNAL, NO. 151)

Story of Joseph

NARRATOR: By means of a pageant, we want to share with you one of the great stories of our faith — the story of a young man who honored his father and through trials and tribulations, and life in a strange land, kept the faith of his father and eventually saved his people from starvation.

(CARD CHOIR TAKES ITS PLACE IN CHOIR LOFT OR IN THE CHANCEL AREA. SPACE SHOULD BE LEFT FOR ACTORS AND PROCESSIONS)

This is the story of Jacob's family. Jacob had twelve sons, but he loved one son, Joseph, more than all the others because he was born to him when he was old. When the other brothers looked at Joseph, they saw "red" from anger.

(BEGIN CARD SET 1: SOME CHOIR MEMBERS HOLD UP RED CARDS)

They were "green" with envy.

(OTHER MEMBERS HOLD UP GREEN CARDS)

They began to feel "blue."

(BLUE CARDS ARE ADDED TO SCENE BY CARD CHOIR)

"What are we, 'yellow' cowards to stand for this?" they asked.

(YELLOW CARDS ADDED)

And their hearts became "black" with evil.

(BLACK CARDS ADDED)

What had caused all these feelings of hatred? It was a special coat that Jacob had given his son Joseph. A long robe with wide sleeves with every color of the rainbow in it.

(ORANGE, PINK, PURPLE CARDS ARE ADDED BY THE CARD CHOIR UNTIL A RAINBOW BACKGROUND IS CREATED)

NARRATOR: (contd) It made the brothers very aware that Joseph was the favorite, the pet, the most loved son. And the brothers cankered with jealousy.

(JOSEPH ENTERS WEARING COAT OF MANY COLORS. STANDS CENTER STAGE. CHOIR LOWERS COLOR CARDS)

And there was more. Joseph fanned the hatred of his brothers by telling them about a dream that he had had.

He said, "Listen to this dream I had. We were all in the field tying up sheaves of wheat, when my sheaf got up and stood up straight. Yours formed a circle around mine and bowed down to it."

(2 YEAR OLDS ENTER, EACH CARRYING A SHEAF OF WHEAT, WHICH MAY BE REAL OR ART WORK. IN ADDITION, THEY MAY HAVE ON BODY COSTUMES. THE CHILDREN FORM A CIRCLE AROUND JOSEPH AND BOW AND SING THE FOLLOWING TO THE TUNE OF "FARMER IN THE DELL")

> We bow to the King
> We bow to the King
> All the wheat within the field
> Will bow to the King.

(CHILDREN EXIT)

NARRATOR: Then the brothers were very angry and said, "Do you think you are going to be a king and rule over us?" And they hated him even more because of his dream and because of what he said about them.

But Joseph was unaware of their hatred, and he had another dream. Quickly he ran to tell his brothers. "I had another dream in which I saw the sun, the moon and eleven stars bowing down to me."

(3 AND 4 YEAR OLDS ENTER. THEY ARE WEARING STAR HEADDRESSES. ALSO, ONE OR MORE WEARS HEADDRESS OF SUN, AND ONE OR MORE WEARS HEADDRESS OF MOON)

(THE CHILDREN CIRCLE JOSEPH AND SING THE FOLLOWING TO THE TUNE OF "FARMER IN THE DELL")

> We bow to the King
> We bow to the King
> Sun and moon and stars above
> All bow to the King.

(CHILDREN BOW AND THEN EXIT)

NARRATOR: "What kind of dream is that?" the brothers said scolding him. "Do you think your father, your mother and your brothers are going to come and bow down to you?" And the brothers began to wish that Joseph was dead.

One day when Joseph's brothers had gone to Shechem to take care of their father's flock, Jacob said to Joseph, "I want you to go to Shechem where your brothers are taking care of the flock."

NARRATOR: (contd) Joseph answered, "I am ready."

The brothers Joseph went to see were:

(BEGIN CARD SET 2: CARD HOLDERS SHOUT NAME AS THEY HOLD UP CARD)

Jacob	Zebuikun
Reuben	Dan
Simeon	Naphtali
Levi	Gad
Judah	Asher
Issachar	

NARRATOR: Joseph's brothers saw him in the distance and before he reached them, they plotted against him and decided to kill him. They said to one another, "Here comes the dreamer. Come on now, let's kill him and throw his body into one of the dry wells. We can say that a wild animal killed him. Then we will see what becomes of his dreams."

(5 YEAR OLDS ENTER, EACH CARRYING A BRICK OR DRESSED AS BRICKS. CHILDREN'S CARDBOARD BUILDING BRICKS ARE GOOD. THEY CIRCLE JOSEPH, KNEEL AND HOLD BRICKS OVER THEIR HEADS, FORMING A WELL AROUND JOSEPH. THEY SING TO TUNE OF "THREE BLIND MICE")

Into the well, Into the well,
Joseph fell, Joseph fell,
The well was deep and held the lad,
His brothers wanted to make him sad,
They put him there 'cause they were bad,
Into the well.

(FIVE YEAR OLDS EXIT)

NARRATOR: While the brothers were debating whether or not to kill Joseph, a caravan of Ishmaelites bound for Egypt passed that way.

(6 AND 7 YEAR OLDS ENTER AS ISHMAELITE PROCESSION FROM BACK OF SANCTUARY. CAMELS CAN BE MADE FROM LONG POLES WITH PAPIER-MACHE CAMEL'S HEADS. CHILDREN RIDING THE CAMELS ARE DRESSED IN ARAB CLOTHING. THEY SLOWLY BOB UP AND DOWN AS THEY COME DOWN THE AISLE. OTHER CHILDREN, IN ARAB DRESS, WALK DOWN AISLE. SOME CARRY POTS AND BASKETS, SOME PLAY TAM-BOURINES. AS THEY COME, THEY SING SUGGESTED SONG: "ZUM GALI GALI GALI," FROM **THE GOOD TIMES SONGBOOK**, ABINGDON PRESS, 1974. ONE CHILD COULD BEAT A DRUM IN A SLOW, MARCHING RHYTHM)

NARRATOR: Joseph's brothers sold him to the Ishmaelites as a slave.

(JOSEPH EXITS WITH ISHMAELITES AS THEY RECESS FROM CHURCH IN THE SAME MANNER AS THEY CAME IN)

Then the brothers dipped his robe in goat's blood and brought it to Jacob, saying that a wild animal had killed Joseph. Jacob tore his clothes in sorrow and put on sackcloth. He felt:

(CARD SET 3: CARD HOLDERS SAY WORD AS THEY HOLD UP CARD)

Discouraged	Miserable
Depressed	Mournful
Sorrowful	Grieving
Disappointed	Downhearted
Unhappy	Gloomy

NARRATOR: And he mourned his son for a long time. Meanwhile, Joseph had arrived in the land of Egypt.

(CARD SET 4: CARD CHOIR FORMS A PICTURE OF EGYPT WITH THE PHAROAH'S PALACE, PALM TREES AND PYRAMIDS IN BACKGROUND, USING A GRID OF 12 CARDS. EACH CARD FORMS A PART OF THE PICTURE AND THEY ARE HELD UP CLOSE TOGETHER. USE THE FOLLOWING ILLUSTRATION AS A GUIDE TO YOUR OWN DRAWING)

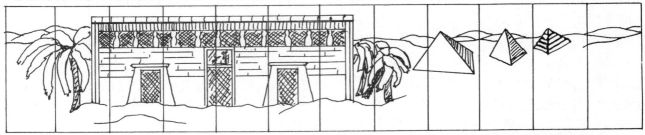

NARRATOR: Joseph had many adventures, but the Lord was always with him and made him successful. Many years passed. He rose to be the most important man in Egypt next to the Pharoah.

(JOSEPH ENTERS IN EGYPTIAN CLOTHING, DOWN AISLE FROM THE BACK OF THE CHURCH IN STATELY PROCESSION. HE TAKES A PLACE DOWN FRONT OF THE CARD PICTURE)

Then a great famine occured in the land of Egypt, but Joseph had predicted this and prepared for it. The famine spread throughout the land and people began to grow very hungry. People came to Egypt from all over the world to buy grain from Joseph. They came from every land.

(8 AND 9 YEAR OLDS ENTER IN ALL SORTS OF COSTUMES IN THE PEOPLE OF THE WORLD PROCESSION. COSTUMES ARE ARAB AND EGYPTIAN, CARRYING FLAGS OF OTHER COUNTRIES IN FRONT OF THEM. THEY COME DOWN THE AISLE AND KNEEL BEFORE JOSEPH. VERY SLOW, SAD PROCESSION TO DIRGE MUSIC)

They came from the North and the South. From the West and the East. They came to Joseph and fell on their knees. For only in Egypt was there grain.

(WHEN THE PROCESSION REACHES JOSEPH, THEY SING, BOWING, AND THEY LEAVE THEIR GIFTS WITH HIM. SING THE FOLLOWING TO TUNE OF BEETHOVEN'S HYMN, "HYMN TO JOY" FOUND IN THE HYMN, "JOYFUL, JOYFUL, WE ADORE THEE," IN THE METHODIST HYMNAL, NO. 38)

Nations come in slow processions,
Tell your land's slow starving pain,
Come to Egypt, humbly bowing
Hoping here to get some grain.   [CONTINUED ON FOLLOWING PAGE]

Bring your money, bring your jewels,

Bring your hopes and bring your fears,

Lay them all in Joseph's keeping,

He can wipe away your tears.

(PROCESSION EXITS AS IT CAME IN)

NARRATOR: Then the sons of Jacob came with the others to buy grain because there was famine in the land of Canaan, too. When Joseph saw his brothers, he recognized them, but they did not recognize him. He looked into their faces. Their hair was gray and their faces lined, but still he recognized:

(REPEAT CARD SET 2: HOLDERS SAY NAME AS THEY HOLD UP CARD)

Jacob	Zebuikun
Reuben	Dan
Simeon	Naphtali
Levi	Gad
Judah	Asher
Issachar	

NARRATOR: "I am your brother Joseph whom you sold into Egypt. Now do not be upset or blame yourself, because you sold me here. It was really God who sent me ahead of you to save people's lives," he said. "Now hurry back to my father and tell him that this is what his son Joseph says, 'God has made me ruler of all Egypt, come to me without delay.'"

But the brothers were filled with fear. "What will he do to us? We deserve his hatred and scorn. If he seeks justice, he can strike us all dead. Heavy is our guilt. What an evil thing we did in selling him – our own brother!"

But Joseph said, "Don't be afraid. God has brought good out of evil, a blessing out of violence and hatred. Now, quickly bring my father to me."

(CARD SET 5: CARD CHOIR WAVES BLANK CARDS TO RIGHT IN UNISON, SAYING, "GO! GO! GO!")

NARRATOR: The brothers left Egypt and went to their father's home in Canaan. When Jacob heard the news, he was stunned and could not believe them. He felt:

(CARD SET 6: CARD HOLDERS SAY WORD AS THEY HOLD UP CARD)

Elated	Joyful
Contented	Happy
Cheerful	Pleased
Delighted	Overjoyed
Gleeful	Exuberant

NARRATOR: "My son Joseph is still alive," he said. "This is all I could ask for. I must go and see him before I die." And they all came — children, grandchildren, sheep, goats, cattle, and everything they had, and Joseph found them homes and farmland and they lived happily for many years.

(CARD SET 7: CARD CHOIR FORMS ACROSTIC AS NARRATOR READS)

CARD 1: P

NARRATOR: Patience had been a part of Joseph's life. Many years he longed to see his father.

CARD 2: R

NARRATOR: Rulers of Egypt and even the Pharoah came to respect him.

CARD 3: A

NARRATOR: Adventures, both good and bad, had marked his path.

CARD 4: I

NARRATOR: Ideals, that he believed in, were never compromised.

CARD 5: S

NARRATOR: Even when he was a slave and a servant, he still served God.

CARD 6: E

NARRATOR: Endurance whether in prison or in a palace was his.

CARD 7: G

NARRATOR: Goodness and honesty were hallmarks of Joseph's character.

CARD 8: O

NARRATOR: Orderliness helped him prepare for the great famine.

CARD 9: D

NARRATOR: Devotion to God was the most important of all.

(CARDS READ "PRAISE GOD")

(CONGREGATION STANDS TO SING)

HYMN: "Doxology" also known as "Praise God From Whom All Blessings Flow" (FOUND IN MOST HYMNALS)

(DURING HYMN, ALL CHARACTERS MAY ASSEMBLE UP FRONT TO TAKE A BOW)

Welcoming New Members to the Church School

INTRODUCTION

This presentation to welcome new members includes all children and parents in the Church School, grades 1 through 6. It can be held in the Fellowship Hall or a large classroom.

PARTICIPANTS

Leader
New Members
Readers 1 and 2
Children and Parents

MATERIALS

song (enclosed)
12" pieces of rope, 1 for each new member
cross with rope tied to it

SOURCES FOR MUSIC SUGGESTIONS

"Hello" — by Ann Price, **Rejoice and Sing Praise,** compiled by Evelyn Andre and Jeneil Menefee, Abingdon Press, 1977.

"Onward Christian Soldiers" — the Methodist Hymnal, No. 305.

"Sing Us One of the Songs of Zion" — music enclosed, page 124.

"We are the Church" — Avery and Marsh, **Rejoice and Sing Praise,** see above.

LITURGY

LEADER: Today we come together for a special occasion — to welcome those who, in the past year, are new to our town or to our Church School. We welcome you!

Saying "Hello" is a beginning. Will you join us in this responsive reading?

CHURCH SCHOOL: We welcome you to our Church School. Hello.

NEW MEMBERS: Hello.

CHURCH SCHOOL: We need your new ideas and suggestions.

NEW MEMBERS: We need your friendship and welcome.

CHURCH SCHOOL: Together we will study —

NEW MEMBERS: And learn —

ALL: And grow!

SONG: "Hello" (BY ANN PRICE, **REJOICE AND SING PRAISE**, ABINGDON PRESS, 1977)

LEADER: "Let us send men before us, that they may explore the land for us, of the way by which we must go up and the cities into which we shall come. They set out and explored and reported, 'It is a good land which the Lord our God gives us.'" (Deut. 1:22-25 Revised Standard Version)

Moving takes a lot of courage. You have to say goodbye to all that is familiar — your friends, the school you were used to, your old house, maybe your special tree or yard. This experience of going with courage into the unknown is a very familiar theme in the Bible. One of the very first stories in our Bible is about a man named Abraham. Abraham, as you may remember, is called the Father of our faith. Let's listen to the Bible story of God calling him.

READER 1: (Genesis 12:1-9) The Lord said to Abram, [who was later to be called Abraham]

READER 2: Leave your native land, your relatives, and your father's home and go to a country that I am going to show you. I will give you many descendants, and they will become a great nation. I will bless you and make your name famous so that you will be a blessing. I will bless those who bless you and I will curse those who curse you. And through you I will bless all the nations.

READER 1: When Abram was seventy-five years old, he started out from Haran, as the Lord had told him to do and Lot went with him. Abram took his wife Sarai, his nephew Lot, and all the wealth and all the slaves they had acquired in Haran, and they started out for the land of Canaan. When they arrived in Canaan, Abram traveled through the land until he came to the sacred tree of Moreh, the holy place at Shechem. (At that time the Canaanites were still living in the land.) The Lord appeared to Abram and said to him:

READER 2: This is the country that I am going to give to your descendants.

READER 1: Then Abram built an altar there to the Lord, who had appeared to him. After that, he moved on south to the hill country, east of the city of Bethel, and set up his camp between Bethel on the west and Ai on the east. There also he built an altar and worshipped the Lord. Then he moved on from place to place, going toward the southern part of Canaan.

LEADER: Like Abraham, we need the courage to face new experiences. Trusting God to guide us as Abraham did, we discover life in ways we never dreamed. If we are willing to let go of the familiar, we discover exciting things in the unmet next moment.

HYMN: "Onward Christian Soldiers" (THE METHODIST HYMNAL, NO. 305)

LEADER: Moving involves loneliness. We have to leave friends we have known for a long time. Sometimes it is hard to make new friends. There are a lot of entrances and exits in our lives. People are constantly coming into our lives or leaving them. Each separation brings its own grief and adjustment.

Let's pause now for a moment and think of all the people who are unhappy because they are lonely and wish they had friends. It is very sad to have no friends. Will you join me in these responsive sentences?

LEADER: For those we left sad,

CONGREGATION: Lord be with them.

LEADER: For not reaching out with a friendly gesture to someone lonely,

CONGREGATION: Lord forgive us.

LEADER: For deliberately ignoring people,

CONGREGATION: Lord have mercy.

LEADER: Father, help us never to forget that we need you and others if we are going to make our world and our church a better place. We ask this through Christ our Lord. Amen.

Again we learn from the Bible that people before us have shared this feeling. Once the people of Israel were captured. Their homes were destroyed and they were forced to march away as captured people into a strange land. Leaving their homes quickly, they gathered up what they could to take with them — some bits of clothing or furnishings. Some, who loved music, gathered their instruments. And then the long sad procession began — shuffling, sobbing people, leaving behind all they had known and moving into a strange, probably hostile new world.

At one time, during the forced march, they rested for a while by a river. As soon as they sat down, they began to cry again as they remembered their homes. Some hung their harps and instruments on nearby trees as they rested. One of the guards saw the instruments and began to taunt the people of Israel. "Hey, sing us one of your songs!" "Come on, let's have a little entertainment!"

And one of the Israelites made the sad reply, "How can we sing the Lord's song in a strange land?" Let's try to experience this story from the Bible together. It is found in the book of Psalms.

First, let's learn this song. Have you ever heard children on the playground tease each other with a sort of sing-song chant? That is what this song is like. As the soldiers taunted the Israelites to sing for them, they might have sounded like this:

SONG: "Sing Us One of the Songs of Zion" (MUSIC ENCLOSED. PRACTICE FIRST LINE)

Now, as we read the story from the Bible, we will pause at a few points and repeat this song, the taunting of the guards.

118

RIGHT SIDE: By the waters of Babylon, there we sat down and wept, when we remembered Zion.

LEFT SIDE: On the willows there we hung up our lyres.

RIGHT SIDE: For there our captors required of us songs and our tormentors, mirth, saying:

ALL SING: "Sing us one of the songs of Zion." (TO ENCLOSED MUSIC AS PRACTICED)

LEFT SIDE: How shall we sing the Lord's song in a foreign land? (MUSIC UNDERNEATH, INCLUDED WITH "SING US ONE OF THE SONGS OF ZION" ENCLOSED)

ALL SING: "Sing us one of the songs of Zion."

RIGHT SIDE: If I forget you, O Jerusalem, let my right hand wither. (MUSIC UNDERNEATH)

ALL SING: "Sing us one of the songs of Zion."

LEFT SIDE: Let my tongue cleave to the roof of my mouth, if I do not remember you. (MUSIC UNDERNEATH)

ALL SING: "Sing us one of the songs of Zion."

RIGHT SIDE: If I do not set Jerusalem above my highest joy! (MUSIC UNDERNEATH)

ALL SING: "Sing us one of the songs of Zion." (Psalms 137:1-6)

LEADER: But the good news which we want to share with you this morning is that you are not in a strange, hostile land like those captured Israelites. You are in a place where we can all sing the Lord's song together. Though you may have come many miles, from places where people talked differently and dressed differently, we worship the same God that you worshipped there and though this particular fellowship may be very different from the one you came from, we are still the same Body of Christ.

Let's pause now and learn about the churches from which our new members came. Will each of our newcomers share with us just a sentence or two about the church from which you came?

(NEWCOMERS JOIN IN SHARING TIME)

You can be proud of how long you were at the church you came from, or how active you were in it. But what is important is that you are called to be the church right here and right now. Each of you has had a different story about the church you came from, but now our stories entwine. You are joining in a new Christian fellowship. Your story of the church will now be the same as ours.

To symbolize this act, I am giving each of our newcomers a piece of rope 12 inches long. On our altar table is a cross with a piece of rope around it. The rope on the cross symbolizes all of us here in this fellowship. Will each of our newcomers come forward and tie their piece of rope onto ours, joining now to be the church in this time and in this place.

(NEWCOMERS TIE ROPES ONTO ROPE AS MUSIC PLAYS IN BACKGROUND, THEN ALL SING)

HYMN: "We Are the Church" (AVERY AND MARSH, **REJOICE AND SING PRAISE**, ABINGDON PRESS, 1977)

SING US ONE OF THE SONGS OF ZION!

Kirk Mariner

SING US ONE OF THE SONGS OF ZI - ON! SING US ONE OF THE SONGS OF ZI - ON!

Background music

Repeat as needed

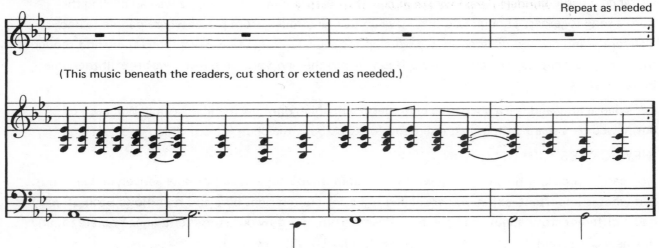

(This music beneath the readers, cut short or extend as needed.)

Music copyright ©1976 by Kirk Mariner. Used by permission.

CLOSING THOUGHTS

Through Special Days in the Church School, we have told the story of our faith. It is a familiar story. It is an on-going story. The more familiar it becomes, the more power we find in it.

Gradually, as the years roll by, we find that in some deep and wonderful way we are a part of this story.

INDEX